# The Book
# of Tea

## Tenshin Okakura

翻訳協力 = ユニカレッジ

序文翻訳 = ジェームス・M・バーダマン

編集協力 = 槇野 修

装　幀 = 寄藤文平　坂野達也

# 茶の本
## The Book of Tea

**Tenshin Okakura**

**岡倉天心＝著**

# 目 次

# CONTENTS

# 生の芸術の響き

　41歳になっていた岡倉天心は、明治35年（1902）
からの５年間に、『東洋の目覚め』『東洋の理想』『日本
の覚醒』『茶の本』という４冊をたてつづけに書いた。
いずれも英文である。なかでも『茶の本』はまるで透
き通った虫の翅のように薄い本であるが、その翅がひ
とたび震えると、日本精神の真髄が遠くまで響いてい
くものになっている。

　天心はこれらの執筆に先立つ20年のあいだ、アーネ
スト・フェノロサとともに東京美術学校を設立し、そ
こを追われ、新たに日本美術院を新設して、紆余曲折が
ありながらもなんとか「日本」や「日本美術」の優秀
性を訴えようとしてきた。

　しかしその訴えは、国内にも、また海外にもほとんど
届いていないという憾みが残っていた。そこで、まずは
アジアのなかの日本の位置を告げ、そのうえで日本の
役割を広く説明しようと試みた。それが上記の３冊に
なったのであるが、その上梓を了えたちょうどそのと
き、日本はロシアと戦って未曾有の勝利をあげるとい
う事態に突入していた。これはひょっとすると、またし
ても日本が誤解を招きかねない。そう感じた天心は、こ
こで一転、日本の心を伝えるには日本人の日々に息づ

# Echoes of an Art of Life

In the five years after he turned forty-one in 1902, Okakura Tenshin published four books one after another: *The Awakening of the East, The Ideals of the East, The Awakening of Japan*, and *The Book of Tea*. All of these were written in English. Among them, *The Book of Tea* is a slight volume, like the diaphanous wings of an insect, and yet once those delicate wings quiver, the essence of the Japanese spirit echoes far and wide.

In the twenty years prior to writing these works, Okakura founded, together with Ernest Fenollosa, the Tokyo Fine Arts School, now Tokyo University of Fine Arts and Music, helped form the Japan Fine Arts Academy, and through many twists and turns, advocated the excellence of Japan and Japanese arts.

Still he remained bitter that what he attempted to call attention to was recognized neither in Japan nor abroad. Therefore, he attempted first to delineate Japan's position within Asia, and then to explain broadly what Japan's role was. This was the purpose of the first three volumes, but shortly following their publication, war broke out between Japan and Russia. The Russo-Japanese War ended in an unprecedented victory for Japan, and that brought forth an entirely new challenge. He became concerned that this

いている美意識や生活感覚をこそ綴ったほうがいいと考えた。こうして生まれたのが、明治39年（1906）にニューヨークで刊行された『茶の本』だったのである。

　構成はまことに絶妙にできている。冒頭、天心は「西洋はいつになったら東洋を理解するのか」という苛立ちを隠していない。そのうえで、西洋がもっぱら「物質」や「理性」を重視するのに対して、日本は「審美」や「内省」を重んじるのだと説明し、その視点をもって読者を茶の世界に誘うように仕向けていった。

　このあと、いくつもの指摘を通して茶の精神を説くのであるが、『茶の本』が今日の多くの茶の湯の案内の本と異なるのは、茶というものが中国の道教や禅を日本独自に変装させた価値観のうえに成り立っているという見方を大前提にして、日本人が茶によっていかに「象徴性と相対性」をこよなく大切にしてきたかというシナリオをちゃんと用意したことだった。

　私が『茶の本』を最初に読んだのは大学生のころであったが、京都の茶室のある呉服屋に育った私にも、この天心の説明はあまりに大胆すぎてついていけなかったものだ。しかし、しだいに私の日本観にも時が熟し、その後は天心の説明こそ今日の日本人にどうしても肝

might bring unexpected misunderstandings regarding Japan. Thinking that in order to communicate the spirit of Japan it would be better to describe the aesthetic and ordinary perceptiveness alive within the Japanese people, Okakura did an about-face. What emerged from this change was *The Book of Tea*, which was published in New York in 1906.

The organization of the volume is superb. In the opening section, Tenshin is unable to conceal his irritation when he writes, "When will the West understand, or try to understand, the East?" He then goes on to contrast the West's exclusive emphasis on material and reason with an explanation of how Japan esteems aesthetic appreciation and introspection. From this perspective, he welcomes and entices the reader into the world of tea.

Following this, he sets forth the spirit of tea by touching on several aspects. What makes *The Book of Tea* different from so many current-day introductions to tea-ceremony is that he offers a carefully outlined argument that tea constitutes the base of a sense of values that was founded in Chinese Taoism and Zen and was created independently in Japan. Upon this major premise, he then argues that the Japanese have, through tea, come to value above all else "Symbolism and Relativity."

The first time I read *The Book of Tea* was when I was a university student. Having grown up in Kyoto in a household selling kimono fabrics and that had its own tea house, I found Tenshin's explanations entirely beyond me. However, as my views of Japan matured, I increasingly

要となるべき骨法をあらわしていると確信できるように
なった。

とくに3つのことを強調しておきたい。第1には、茶
が「生の芸術」で、それゆえつねに「現在」と向き合
うものだとしたことだ。それを説明するために天心は、
茶には始めも終わりもないと書いた。

第2には、茶においては自己の超越がおこりうると
したことだ。これは西洋の理性的自己をいささか意図
的に揶揄しているきらいはあるものの、まさに天心が
主張しておきたい汎東洋的な「無の介在」を訴えるには、
どうしても欠かせない説明だったろう。

第3に、これが私には最も響きつづけているメッセー
ジになるのだが、茶を通して日本人は、実は「不完全」
を学んでいるのだと喝破した。不完全に学ぶというの
は、どんなことであれ、すべてを仕上がったものとはみ
なさないで、そこにいくばくかの想像力を補って臨む
という意味である。

注意深く読んでいくと、『茶の本』には一首の和歌と
一句の俳句が紹介されていることがわかる。

> 見渡せば
> 花ももみぢも
> なかりけり
> 浦の苦屋の
> 秋の夕暮

became convinced that Tenshin's explanations manifested the fundamental, vital underpinnings of the Japanese today.

There are three points in his work that I would like to call attention to. First is that tea is "an Art of Life," and therefore it is always in touch with the present. Tenshin writes that in tea, this has no beginning and no end.

He also shows that through tea one can transcend the self. While this may smack of a slightly deliberate ridicule of the West's rational self, it would seem to be rather an essential aspect in Tenshin's argument for a broadly Eastern "Abode of Vacancy," or the mediacy of emptiness.

Thirdly—and this is the message that echoes so strongly within me—he has astutely observed that it was through tea that the Japanese learned the value of "incompleteness." Regardless of the specific case in question, to learn something "incompletely" means not to equate everything as complete in and of itself but to deal with it with a certain supplementary imagination.

Upon close reading, one will discover that a waka and a haiku are introduced in the text.

> *I looked beyond;*
> *Flowers are not,*
> *Nor tinted leaves.*
> *On the sea beach*
> *A solitary cottage stands*
> *In the waning light*
> *Of an autumn eve.*

夕月夜
海すこしある
木の間かな

　いずれも千利休や小堀遠州がこれをもって茶の心だとみなした歌と句であるが、ここには眼前に見える光景が不完全であるからこそ、そこにかえって無限の想像力がはたらいていくのだという感慨が、含意と余情をもってうたわれている。天心もそのことが言いたくて、この一冊を構成したと言っていいほどである。

　天心が『茶の本』で説いたことは、茶道の作法や心得ではなかった。茶道という「生の芸術」をもつにいたった日本人の、その培われた精神の構想のあらましを説こうとした。おそらくはざっと読めば数時間もかからない一冊であろうけれど、この一冊が日本人に、また外国人にもたらすものは、いまなおはかりしれない響きをもっている。

松岡正剛

*A cluster of summer trees,*
*A bit of the sea,*
*A pale evening moon.*

Sen no Rikiu and Kobori-Enshiu, respectively, claimed that each poem conveyed the spirit of tea. In these poems, the fact that the scene before one is incomplete implies and suggests that unlimited powers of imagination are at work. If anything, this is what Tenshin hoped to say in writing this book.

What Tenshin was setting forth in *The Book of Tea* was not instructions on tea-ceremony or etiquette. Rather, he was propounding an outline of the spiritual make-up cultivated within the Japanese people through the way of tea as "an Art of Living." This book can easily be read straight through in a few hours, and yet it is a volume that even today brings to both Japanese and non-Japanese profound reverberations.

Seigow MATSUOKA

# 第 1 章　心の器

# Chapter 1　The Cup of Humanity

茶ははじめ薬として用いられ、やがて飲み物となった。8世紀の中国では、高尚な遊びのひとつとして詩歌の世界に取り入れられた。さらに15世紀になると、日本において喫茶は審美的な信仰にまで高められ**茶道**が生まれたのである。茶道は、日常の俗境のなかに美をみいだし、それを賛美する心に基づいた一種の儀式である。そして茶道は、純粋、調和、たがいを思いやる慈愛心の深さ、社会秩序の理想といったものを教えてくれる。その根本は、「**不完全なもの**」を敬う心にあり、ままならない人生にあって、可能なことだけでもやってみようという心優しい挑戦なのだ。

　茶の思想は、いわゆる**審美主義**という言葉で片づけられるほど単純ではない。そこには、倫理や宗教とともに、あらゆる側面から、人間と自然との関わり合いをみることができる。清潔を厳しく求められる点で衛生学、手間と金をかけず簡素に楽しむという点で経済学、宇宙に対するモノの大きさが分かるという点で精神の幾何学ともいえる。そして、茶をたしなむことで誰でも趣味上の貴族になり得るという点で東洋的民主主義の本質をあらわしているのである。

　日本が鎖国によって、世界から長く孤立していたことは、独自の感性を見極めることの助け

Tea began as a medicine and grew into a beverage. In China, in the eighth century, it entered the realm of poetry as one of the polite amusements. The fifteenth century saw Japan ennoble it into a religion of æstheticism—**Teaism**. Teaism is a cult founded on the adoration of the beautiful among the sordid facts of everyday existence. It inculcates purity and harmony, the mystery of mutual charity, the romanticism of the social order. It is essentially a worship of the **Imperfect**, as it is a tender attempt to accomplish something possible in this impossible thing we know as life.

The Philosophy of Tea is not mere **æstheticism** in the ordinary acceptance of the term, for it expresses conjointly with ethics and religion our whole point of view about man and nature. It is hygiene, for it enforces cleanliness; it is economics, for it shows comfort in simplicity rather than in the complex and costly; it is moral geometry, inasmuch as it defines our sense of proportion to the universe. It represents the true spirit of Eastern democracy by making all its votaries aristocrats in taste.

The long isolation of Japan from the rest of the world, so conducive to introspection, has been highly

となり、茶道は大きく発展していった。私たちの住まい、習慣、衣食、陶器や漆器、絵画、そして文学に至るまですべてに茶道の影響がみられる。日本文化の研究をするものは茶道の存在を無視することはできないだろう。茶道の精神は貴人の閨房（けいぼう）から蓬屋（ほうおく）にいたるまで広く染み渡っている。わが国の農民は花を活ける術（すべ）を知っており、みすぼらしい人夫さえ山水を愛でる心得がある。よく「あの人には**茶気がない**」という言い方をするが、これは人生の微妙な情感に無神経な人をさす表現である。また、現実の悲しい出来事に無頓着で、浮かれはしゃいでいる手のつけられないお調子者は「**お茶らけ**」といって非難される。

▶ **閨房**
寝室の意。

▶ **蓬屋**
あばら屋、みすぼらしい家の意。

傍（かたわ）らから見れば何でもないことをわざわざ面倒くさくしているのだから、不思議に思うかもしれない。たかが茶の一杯に、なんと大げさなというであろう。しかし、人間の喜びを入れる器は、なにしろ小さくて、涙を流せばすぐに溢れてしまい、とまらぬ渇きを潤そうとすれば、すぐに飲み干せるほどであることを思えば、たかが茶碗をありがたがるくらいで、責められることもなかろう。人間の過ちはもっと別のところにある。われわれは酒の神バッカスに惜しげもなく犠牲を捧げたり、軍神マルスの姿を借りた血なまぐさい闘いを美化したりした。それに比べれば、カメリアの女神に惚れ込んで、祭壇から流れでる温かな思いやりの心に浸るぐらいいいではない

▶ **バッカス**
ギリシア神話の酒の神。ディオニュソスの別名。

▶ **マルス**
ローマ神話の戦いの神。擬人化して戦争の意味。

▶ **カメリア**
ツバキ。茶がツバキ科に属することから茶を意味する比喩表現。

favourable to the development of Teaism. Our home and habits, costume and cuisine, porcelain, lacquer, painting—our very literature—all have been subject to its influence. No student of Japanese culture could ever ignore its presence. It has permeated the elegance of noble boudoirs, and entered the abode of the humble. Our peasants have learned to arrange flowers, our meanest labourer to offer his salutation to the rocks and waters. In our common parlance we speak of the man "**with no tea**" in him, when he is insusceptible to the seriocomic interests of the personal drama. Again we stigmatise the untamed æsthete who, regardless of the mundane tragedy, runs riot in the springtide of emancipated emotions, as one "**with too much tea**" in him.

The outsider may indeed wonder at this seeming much ado about nothing. What a tempest in a tea-cup! he will say. But when we consider how small after all the cup of human enjoyment is, how soon overflowed with tears, how easily drained to the dregs in our quenchless thirst for infinity, we shall not blame ourselves for making so much of the tea-cup. Mankind has done worse. In the worship of Bacchus, we have sacrificed too freely; and we have even transfigured the gory image of Mars. Why not consecrate ourselves to the queen of the Camelias, and revel in the warm stream of sympathy that flows from her altar? In the liquid amber within the ivory-porcelain, the initiated may touch the sweet reticence of **Confucius**,

か？　ひとたび足を踏み入れれば、白磁に注がれた液体の琥珀色を通して、**孔子**の心休まる沈黙や**老子**の気の利いた言葉、そして**釈迦**の優美な香気に触れることができるだろう。

　自分にとっての大事がじつは小事なのだと気づかない人間は、他人の小事がじつは大事だということを見過ごしがちである。一般の西洋人は**茶の湯**をみて、東洋の数ある奇妙で子供じみた風習のひとつにすぎないと軽く考えていることだろう。彼らは日本人が平和に芸術にふけっているときは野蛮な国だとみなしていたが、満州戦線で大量殺戮をはじめると、文明国と呼ぶようになった。最近は**武士道**——わが兵士が自らを犠牲にして戦う「死の術」——についてよく話題になるが、紛れもなく「生の術」である茶道には露ほどの光も当たらない。もし、おぞましい戦争の栄光が文明国の証しなら、われわれは喜んで野蛮人のままでいよう。われわれの芸術や理想に当然の敬意が払われるようになるまで、喜んで待つことにしよう。

　西洋はいつになったら東洋を理解するのだろう、いや、理解しようとするのだろうか？　われわれアジア人は、虚実をない交ぜにしてつくり上げられた、自分たちに関する奇妙な話にしばしば愕然とすることがある。鼠や油虫とまではいかなくとも、蓮の香りをかいで生きていると言われたりする。あり得ない狂言か、卑屈な思い

▶**日露戦争**
　1904-05、日本とロシアが満州の制覇を争った戦争。そのすぐ後、1906年に『茶の本』は出版されている。

the piquancy of **Laotse**, and the ethereal aroma of **Sakyamuni** himself.

Those who cannot feel the littleness of great things in themselves are apt to overlook the greatness of little things in others. The average Westerner, in his sleek complacency, will see in the **tea-ceremony** but another instance of the thousand and one oddities which constitute the quaintness and childishness of the East to him. He was wont to regard Japan as barbarous while she indulged in the gentle arts of peace: he calls her civilised since she began to commit wholesale slaughter on Manchurian battlefields. Much comment has been given lately to the **Code of the Samurai,**—the **Art of Death** which makes our soldiers exult in self-sacrifice; but scarcely any attention has been drawn to Teaism, which represents so much of our **Art of Life**. Fain would we remain barbarians, if our claim to civilisation were to be based on the gruesome glory of war. Fain would we await the time when due respect shall be paid to our art and ideals.

When will the West understand, or try to understand, the East? We Asiatics are often appalled by the curious web of facts and fancies which has been woven concerning us. We are pictured as living on the perfume of the lotus, if not on mice and cockroaches. It is either impotent fanaticism or else abject voluptuousness. Indian spirituality has been derided as ignorance,

込みだ。インドの霊性を無知とあざけり、中国の謹直を愚鈍と笑い、日本人の愛国心を**宿命論**の産物だとののしる。われわれは神経組織が鈍感なため、痛みや傷がわからないとまでいわれてきたのだ！

　われわれを虚仮(こけ)にして楽しむといい。アジアも返礼する。あなた方についてわれわれがどう想像し、どう書き記してきたかを知ったら、さらなるお楽しみの種になるだろう。われわれは、はるか彼方に見えるものへのあこがれ、未知なものに対する無意識の崇拝、そして目新しいものや判断のつかないものへの敵意を西洋人に対して抱いてきた。あなた方は、他人が羨んでも足りないくらい立派な徳を背負い、とがめる気持ちも失せるほど派手な罪も犯している。わが国の昔の文人、つまり物知りが、西洋人は服の下に毛むくじゃらのしっぽを隠していて、生まれたての赤ん坊の肉を煮込み料理にして食しているなどと言っていた。いや、われわれはあなた方に対してさらに悪いイメージを持っていた。「西洋人ほど実践したこともないことを説教する、口先ばかりの人間はいない」と思っていたのである。

　しかしこのような誤解は急速に解消されつつある。商取引きが盛んになり、東洋の港では西洋の言葉を使わざるを得なくなっているし、アジアの若者たちは近代的な教育を求めて西洋の大学に群がっている。かの地の文化を深く理解することは無理としても、何はともあれ進んで学ぼうとしている。日本人のなかには、堅い衿(カラー)やシ

Chinese sobriety as stupidity, Japanese patriotism as the result of **fatalism**. It has been said that we are less sensible to pain and wounds on account of the callousness of our nervous organisation!

Why not amuse yourselves at our expense? Asia returns the compliment. There would be further food for merriment if you were to know all that we have imagined and written about you. All the glamour of the perspective is there, all the unconscious homage of wonder, all the silent resentment of the new and undefined. You have been loaded with virtues too refined to be envied, and accused of crimes too picturesque to be condemned. Our writers in the past—the wise men who knew—informed us that you had bushy tails somewhere hidden in your garments, and often dined off a fricassee of newborn babes! Nay, we had something worse against you: we used to think you the most impracticable people on the earth, for you were said to preach what you never practised.

Such misconceptions are fast vanishing amongst us. Commerce has forced the European tongues on many an Eastern port. Asiatic youths are flocking to Western colleges for the equipment of modern education. Our insight does not penetrate your culture deeply, but at least we are willing to learn. Some of my compatriots have adopted too much of your customs and too much

ルクハットを身につければ西洋文明に近づけると勘違いし、西洋の習慣や作法を真似するばかりの輩もいる。こうした様相は嘆かわしいかぎりだが、それはひざまづいても西洋に追いつきたいとするわれわれの気持ちのあらわれでもある。それにひきかえ、西洋の人々は東洋に対してうしろ向きだ。**キリスト教の宣教師**は分け与えることはしても、受け入れることはしない。あなた方が持っている情報は、通りすがりの旅人からの聞きかじりの話とは言わないまでも、われらの膨大な書籍の貧弱な翻訳に基づくものでしかない。ラフカディオ・ハーンの騎士道的な見地に立って書かれた著作や、『インド生活の仕組み』の著者のように、われわれの心の機微を理解しながら未知なる**東洋の神秘**を照らし出した例はまれである。

このようなあけすけな物言いをすると、私自身が**茶道**のことなど何も分かっていないと自ら露呈しているようなものかもしれない。他人が言ってほしいと期待している以上のことは口にしないという**礼節**こそが茶道の精神なのだから。もっとも私自身、立派な**茶人**のつもりはない。新旧両世界は、互いの誤解によってすでに多くの傷を負っているのだから、より深い理解を促すためにほんの少し肩を押したからといって弁明する必要はないだろう。20世紀初めの血なまぐさい戦争も、ロシアがもっとへりくだって日本をよく知ろうとしていれば、避けられたはずだ。東洋の問題を軽んじて無視するなら、人類にはそ

▶**ラフカディオ・ハーン**
　1850–1904、小泉八雲の本名。1890年に来日し、『心』『怪談』など日本に関する英文の著作を発表。

▶**『インド生活の仕組み』**
　岡倉天心著『東洋の理想』の序文を書いたことで知られるニヴェディタ(本名マーガレット・ノーブル)の代表作。

of your etiquette, in the delusion that the acquisition of stiff collars and tall silk hats comprised the attainment of your civilisation. Pathetic and deplorable as such affectations are, they evince our willingness to approach the West on our knees. Unfortunately the Western attitude is unfavourable to the understanding of the East. The **Christian missionary** goes to impart, but not to receive. Your information is based on the meagre translations of our immense literature, if not on the unreliable anecdotes of passing travellers. It is rarely that the chivalrous pen of a Lafcadio Hearn or that of the author of *The Web of Indian Life* enlivens the **Oriental darkness** with the torch of our own sentiments.

Perhaps I betray my own ignorance of the **Tea Cult** by being so outspoken. Its very **spirit of politeness** exacts that you say what you are expected to say, and no more. But I am not to be a polite **Teaist**. So much harm has been done already by the mutual misunderstanding of the New World and the Old, that one need not apologise for contributing his tithe to the furtherance of a better understanding. The beginning of the twentieth century would have been spared the spectacle of sanguinary warfare if Russia had condescended to know Japan better. What dire consequences to humanity lie in the contemptuous ignoring of Eastern problems! European imperialism, which does not disdain to raise

▶黄禍
　黄色人種が白色
人種を脅かすとい
う禍害。

▶白禍
　白色人種が黄色
人種を脅かすとい
う禍害。

ら恐ろしい結果が待っているであろう。ヨーロッパの帝国主義は「黄禍」というばかげた言葉を声高に叫んでいる一方で、アジアが「残忍な白禍」を意識し始めていることに気づきもしない。われわれには「茶気がありすぎる」といってあなた方は笑うかもしれないが、西洋の人々は生来「茶気」を持ち合わせていないのではなかろうか。

　互いに警句をとばし合うのはもう止めにしよう。両半球が互いに歩み寄る賢明さがあれば、憂いもなくなろう。われわれは今まで違う方向に進んできた。だからといって互いに相手を補えない理由はないはずだ。あなた方は心の安定を失ってまで膨張を遂げた。われわれは侵略に対して無力だが、調和をつくり出した。どうだろう？東洋はある意味、西洋よりも尊敬に値しないだろうか？

　不思議なことに、茶碗のなかではすでに十分なほど東西の心が触れあってきた。茶道こそ世界に受け入れられた唯一のアジアの儀式である。白人は、われわれの宗教や道徳を嘲笑してきたものの、褐色の飲み物はあっさりと受け入れたのだ。午後の喫茶は、今や西洋社会に欠かせない役割を果たしている。カップと受け皿が触れあう微妙な音や、心を込めてもてなす女性の優しい衣擦れの音、そしてクリームや砂糖についての何気ないやりとりに「お茶への礼賛」がしっかりと根づいていることが分かる。これから出される煎茶がどんな加減かわからなくても、運を

the absurd cry of the **Yellow Peril,** fails to realise that Asia may also awaken to the cruel sense of the **White Disaster**. You may laugh at us for having "too much tea," but may we not suspect that you of the West have "no tea" in your constitution?

Let us stop the continents from hurling epigrams at each other, and be sadder if not wiser by the mutual gain of half a hemisphere. We have developed along different lines, but there is no reason why one should not supplement the other. You have gained expansion at the cost of restlessness; we have created a harmony which is weak against aggression. Will you believe it?—the East is better off in some respects than the West!

Strangely enough humanity has so far met in the tea-cup. It is the only Asiatic ceremonial which commands universal esteem. The white man has scoffed at our religion and our morals, but has accepted the brown beverage without hesitation. The afternoon tea is now an important function in Western society. In the delicate clatter of trays and saucers, in the soft rustle of feminine hospitality, in the common catechism about cream and sugar, we know that the **Worship of Tea** is established beyond question. The philosophic resignation of the guest to the fate awaiting him in the dubious decoction proclaims that in this single instance

天に任せてあわてない、これこそ東洋の精神が最高に発揮される瞬間である。

ヨーロッパにおけるお茶についての最古の記録は、アラブ人旅行者の記述に見られ、西暦879年以後、広東の主要な収入源は塩と茶の税金だったと書かれている。マルコ・ポーロの記録によれば、中国の蔵相が茶の税金を不当に値上げしたため、1285年に免職になっている。ヨーロッパの人々が極東についてさらによく知るようになったのは**大航海時代**のことである。16世紀の終わり、オランダ人は東洋では灌木の葉からさわやかな飲料がつくられていると伝えている。ジョバンニ・バチスタ・ラムシオ（1559年）、L・アルメディア（1576年）、マフェノ（1588年）、タレイラ（1610年）なども茶についての記述を残している。1610年、オランダ東インド会社の船が最初の茶をヨーロッパにもたらした。1636年、それがフランスに伝わり、1638年にはロシアにまで広がった。1650年にはイギリスが嬉々としてこれを受け入れ、「この素晴らしく美味で、医者も推奨する中国の飲み物は、中国語で〈Tcha〉といい、その他の国では〈Tay〉もしくは〈Tee〉というらしい」などと評判になった。

この世の優れたものが決まってそうであるように、茶にも反対意見を唱えるものがでた。ヘンリー・サヴィル（1678年）というへそまがりは、喫茶を不潔な習慣として公然と非難した。ジョナス・ハンウェイ（『茶の話』1756年）にいたっては、茶を飲むと男は背が縮み、男ぶりが落ち、

▶**大航海時代**
　15世紀から17世紀前半にかけ、ヨーロッパ人が新航路、大陸を探し、活発に海外進出した時代。

▶**灌木**
　低い木のこと。

▶**オランダ東インド会社**
　1602年、東洋との貿易のためオランダに設立された会社。植民地経営にも携わった。

the Oriental spirit reigns supreme.

The earliest record of tea in European writing is said to be found in the statement of an Arabian traveller, that after the year 879 the main sources of revenue in Canton were the duties on salt and tea. Marco Polo records the deposition of a Chinese minister of finance in 1285 for his arbitrary augmentation of the tea-taxes. It was at the period of the **great discoveries** that the European people began to know more about the extreme Orient. At the end of the sixteenth century the Hollanders brought the news that a pleasant drink was made in the East from the leaves of a bush. The travellers Giovanni Batista Ramusio (1559), L. Almeida (1576), Maffeno (1588), Tareira (1610), also mentioned tea. In the last-named year ships of the Dutch East India Company brought the first tea into Europe. It was known in France in 1636, and reached Russia in 1638. England welcomed it in 1650 and spoke of it as "That excellent and by all physicians approved China drink, called by the Chineans Tcha, and by other nations Tay, alias Tee."

Like all the good things of the world, the propaganda of Tea met with opposition. Heretics like Henry Saville (1678) denounced drinking it as a filthy custom. Jonas Hanway (*Essay on Tea*, 1756) said that men seemed to lose their stature and comeliness, women their beauty through the use of tea. Its cost at

女は美を損なうだろうといっている。最初のうちは、茶は非常に高価（1ポンドで15〜16シリング）だったので、庶民には手の届かない品だった。代わりに王室の特別のもてなしや楽しみ、貴族の贈答品として用いられた。だが、こうした**不利な条件**をものともせず、喫茶はまたたく間に広まっていった。18世紀の前半には、ロンドンのコーヒーハウスが、事実上、ティーハウスになり、アディソンやスティールといった**才人**は「お茶一杯」を楽しむためにそこへ通いつめた。この飲物はまもなく生活必需品となり、税金の対象となった。ここで思い出すのが、近代史における茶の重要な役割についてである。圧政下にあった植民地アメリカは、茶の重税に耐えられなくなり、ボストン港に茶箱を投げ捨てた。その日から**アメリカの独立**が始まったのである。

　茶の味にはとらえがたい魅力があり、人はこれに惹かれて理想の茶を追求したくなる。西洋の粋人たちが、えもいわれぬ茶の香りを、自分たちの思想にとりこむのにそう時間はかからなかった。茶はワインのように勿体ぶっていないし、コーヒーのような自意識もなく、ココアのような無邪気な気取りもない。1711年、イギリスの新聞スペクテイター紙はすでに、こんな謳い文句を使っている。「毎朝1時間かけて、お茶、パン、バターという朝食を頂く、規則正しい生活をおくるご家庭にこそ、この新聞をお茶の支度のひと品として食卓にご用意くださることをお勧めいたします」サミュエル・ジョンソンは自

▶**ボストン茶会事件**
　1773年、イギリスの制定した条例に反対して起きた事件。

▶**サミュエル・ジョンソン**
　1709–1784、シェイクスピアの研究などで知られるイギリスの文学者。

the start (about fifteen or sixteen shillings a pound) forbade popular consumption, and made it "regalia for high treatments and entertainments, presents being made thereof to princes and grandees." Yet in spite of such **drawbacks** tea-drinking spread with marvellous rapidity. The coffeehouses of London in the early half of the eighteenth century became, in fact, tea-houses, the resort of **wits** like Addison and Steele, who beguiled themselves over their "dish of tea." The beverage soon became a necessary of life—a taxable matter. We are reminded in this connection what an important part it plays in modern history. Colonial America resigned herself to oppression until human endurance gave way before the heavy duties laid on Tea. **American independence** dates from the throwing of tea-chests into Boston harbour.

There is a subtle charm in the taste of tea which makes it irresistible and capable of idealisation. Western humourists were not slow to mingle the fragrance of their thought with its aroma. It has not the arrogance of wine, the self-consciousness of coffee, nor the simpering innocence of cocoa. Already in 1711, says the *Spectator*: "I would therefore in a particular manner recommend these my speculations to all well-regulated families that set apart an hour every morning for tea, bread and butter; and would earnestly advise them for their good to order this paper to be punctually served up and to be looked upon as a part of the tea-equipage." Samuel Johnson draws his own portrait as "a hardened and

らを表現してこう言っている。「恥も外聞もない大の茶飲みで、20年もの間、この魅惑的な植物の煎じ液だけで食べ物を流し込んできた。茶とともに宵を楽しみ、夜更けに茶で癒やされ、茶とともに朝を迎えた」

茶の信奉者として知られているチャールズ・ラムは、「密かに善行をなし、それが偶然に知れる。これこそ私の知る最大の喜びである」と茶道の真髄を表現している。茶道は美を巧みに隠し、それを見つける術であり、あからさまにせず、ほのめかす術である。自らを冷静に、しかも笑いの的にする高尚なテクニックである。ゆえに茶道はユーモアそのものであり、**達観の笑み**なのだ。ということは、真の粋人はみな、茶人といえるのかもしれない。たとえばサッカレー、そして、いうまでもなくシェイクスピア。デカダンスの詩人たち（堕落していない世の中などあるだろうか？）は**物質主義**への抵抗という意味で茶道への道をわずかに開いた。おそらく今日では、この不完全なものを冷静にじっくりと眺めることで、東西が互いに慰め合えるのではないだろうか。

**道教の徒**によれば、「**無始**」という大いなる始まりのときに、「心」と「物」が決死の戦いをし、ついに「大日輪黄帝」が闇と地の邪神である「祝融」に勝利した。負けた巨人は断末魔の苦しみにのたうちまわり、頭を天涯にぶつけて硬玉の青天井を粉砕してしまった。星々は居場所を失い、月は荒涼たる夜空をあてどなくさまよった。困り果てた黄帝は、遠く広く天の修理人を探し

▶チャールズ・ラム
1775–1834、イギリスの文学作家。『シェイクスピア物語』の著者として有名。イギリスの東インド会社に勤務したこともある。

▶祝融
中国神話の火と南方を司る神。

shameless tea-drinker, who for twenty years diluted his meals with only the infusion of the fascinating plant; who with tea amused the evening, with tea solaced the midnight, and with tea welcomed the morning."

Charles Lamb, a professed devotee, sounded the true note of Teaism when he wrote that the greatest pleasure he knew was to do a good action by stealth, and to have it found out by accident. For Teaism is the art of concealing beauty that you may discover it, of suggesting what you dare not reveal. It is the noble secret of laughing at yourself, calmly yet thoroughly, and is thus humour itself,—the **smile of philosophy**. All genuine humourists may in this sense be called tea philosophers,—Thackeray, for instance, and, of course, Shakespeare. The poets of the Decadence (when was not the world in decadence?), in their protests against **materialism**, have, to a certain extent, also opened the way to Teaism. Perhaps nowadays it is in our demure contemplation of the Imperfect that the West and the East can meet in mutual consolation.

The **Taoists** relate that at the great beginning of the **No-Beginning**, Spirit and Matter met in mortal combat. At last the Yellow Emperor, the Sun of Heaven, triumphed over Shuhyung, the demon of darkness and earth. The Titan, in his death agony, struck his head against the solar vault and shivered the blue dome of jade into fragments. The stars lost their nests, the moon wandered aimlessly among the wild

▶**女媧**
　祝融と戦った神
話上の女神。

求めた。その甲斐あって、東の海から女神「女
媧」が、角をはやし、竜の尾を持ち、炎の鎧に身
を包んで煌然とあらわれた。この女神は、五色の
虹を不思議な大窯で溶かし、中国の天空を造り
直した。ところが女媧はこのとき、青天に残され
たふたつの穴を埋め忘れた。これが**愛の二元論**
の始まりで、ふたつの魂は空間を流転し、力を合
わせて宇宙を完成させるまでとどまることがで
きないという。人は誰しも希望と平和を求めて、
自らの天空を造り直さねばならないのである。

　現代社会に生きる人類の天空は、彼の巨人の
ように富と権力を求める戦いのなかで、粉々に
砕かれている。世界は**利己主義**と**俗悪趣味**の闇
に漂っている。知は悪意によって用いられ、**仁**は
功利のためにおこなわれている。東西世界は荒
れ狂う海に放り出された2匹の竜のように、人
生の宝玉を取り戻そうともがいているが、無駄
なことである。この巨大な廃墟を修復するには

▶**アヴァターラ**
　ヒンドゥー教の
救済の神の化身。

女媧の再来が不可欠なのだ。我々はアヴァター
ラを待っている。さてその間に、一服、お茶でも
いかがだろう。昼下がりの陽光に竹林がきらめ
いている。泉はいきいきと沸き返り、松韻が釜に
響く。儚さを夢にみて、美しく、されど、取りと
めのないことに時間をゆだねてみよう。

chasms of the night. In despair the Yellow Emperor sought far and wide for the repairer of the Heavens. He had not to search in vain. Out of the Eastern sea rose a queen, the divine Niuka, horn-crowned and dragon-tailed, resplendent in her armour of fire. She welded the five-coloured rainbow in her magic cauldron and rebuilt the Chinese sky. But it is also told that Niuka forgot to fill two tiny crevices in the blue firmament. Thus began the **dualism of love**—two souls rolling through space and never at rest until they join together to complete the universe. Everyone has to build anew his sky of hope and peace.

The heaven of modern humanity is indeed shattered in the Cyclopean struggle for wealth and power. The world is groping in the shadow of **egotism** and **vulgarity**. Knowledge is bought through a bad conscience, **benevolence** practised for the sake of utility. The East and West, like two dragons tossed in a sea of ferment, in vain strive to regain the jewel of life. We need a Niuka again to repair the grand devastation; we await the great Avatar. Meanwhile, let us have a sip of tea. The afternoon glow is brightening the bamboos, the fountains are bubbling with delight, the soughing of the pines is heard in our kettle. Let us dream of evanescence, and linger in the beautiful foolishness of things.

第 **2** 章 茶の流派

Chapter 2 The Schools of Tea

茶は芸術品であるから、その高貴な味わいを引き出すには名人の手を必要とする。絵画に傑作と駄作があるように——たいていは後者だが——茶にも善し悪しがある。完璧な茶を点(た)てるための秘訣などは存在しない。ティツィアーノや雪村の絵を描く工程に決まりがないのと同じことである。茶葉の調整にもそれぞれ独自の仕方があり、水や熱との相性も、先祖伝来の秘法も、独自の言い回しもさまざまである。真の美とは常にそういうところに存在するのに違いない。芸術と人生のこの簡素にして根本的な法則は、社会の怠慢によってずっと見過ごされてきたため、それによってわれわれはどれだけの損失をこうむってきたことだろう。宋の詩人李竹嬾(り ちくらん)は、この世には最も嘆かわしいことが3つあると述べている。誤った教育によって優れた若人の前途を損なうこと、低俗な鑑賞法で素晴しい絵画の価値を下げること、そして淹(い)れ方を誤って素晴らしい茶を台なしにしてしまうこと、である。

芸術と同じく、茶にも時代と流派がある。茶の発展はおおよそ3つの段階に分けられる。**団茶**（固形茶を煮るもの）、**抹茶**（粉茶）、**煎茶**（淹茶(だしちゃ)）である。現代は煎茶の時代である。これらの茶の味わい方は、それぞれの茶が流行した時代の精神をあらわしている。日々の生活には、われわれ

▶ティツィアーノ
1490–1576、ルネサンス期のイタリアの画家。

▶雪村
1504–1589、室町後期の水墨画家。

Tea is a work of art and needs a master hand to bring out its noblest qualities. We have good and bad tea, as we have good and bad paintings—generally the latter. There is no single recipe for making the perfect tea, as there are no rules for producing a Titian or a Sesson. Each preparation of the leaves has its individuality, its special affinity with water and heat, its hereditary memories to recall, its own method of telling a story. The truly beautiful must be always in it. How much do we not suffer through the constant failure of society to recognise this simple and fundamental law of art and life; Lichihlai, a Sung poet, has sadly remarked that there were three most deplorable things in the world: the spoiling of fine youths through false education, the degradation of fine paintings through vulgar admiration, and the utter waste of fine tea through incompetent manipulation.

Like Art, Tea has its periods and its schools. Its evolution may be roughly divided into three main stages: the **Boiled Tea**, the **Whipped Tea**, and the **Steeped Tea**. We moderns belong to the last school. These several methods of appreciating the beverage are indicative of the spirit of the age in which they

の無意識からおこる行動や、心の奥底にあるものが常に映し出されるからである。孔子いわく「人いずくんぞかくさんや（人は隠しおおすことができない）」。われわれが些細な事柄に自己を顕してしまうのは、おそらく内に秘めた偉大なものをほとんど持っていないためではないだろうか。日々の些末な出来事も、高尚な哲学や詩歌と同じく、民族の理想を知るための手がかりとなるのである。ワインの好みの違いが、ヨーロッパ諸国の時代精神の特徴をそれぞれ示しているように、どんな茶を理想とするかということに、東洋文化のさまざまな気風が特徴づけられているのだ。煮て飲む固形の**団茶**、泡立てて飲む**抹茶**、煎じて飲む**煎茶**のそれぞれが、中国の唐、宋、明の異なる気質をはっきりと示している。昨今濫用されている芸術分類の用語を借りれば、これらをそれぞれ**古典派、ロマン派、自然主義派**の茶といってもよい。

▶**唐**（618–907）
**宋**（960–1279）
**明**（1368–1644）
中国歴代の王朝。

　中国南部の原産である茶の木は、植物学としても薬学としてもきわめて早い時期から知られていた。古典のなかでは「茶<ruby>た</ruby>」、「蔎<ruby>せつ</ruby>」、「荈<ruby>せん</ruby>」、「檟<ruby>か</ruby>」、「茗<ruby>みょう</ruby>」などのさまざまな名で記録されており、疲労回復、精神の高揚、意志の強化、視力回復などに優れた効能があるとされていた。内服薬として用いられるだけでなく、しばしば軟膏としてリューマチの痛みを和らげるのに外用薬として使われていた。道教の徒は茶を**不老不死の霊薬**の主成分であるとしていた。仏教徒は長時間の瞑想中の眠気覚ましとして、広く茶を服用

prevailed. For life is an expression, our unconscious actions the constant betrayal of our innermost thought. Confucius said that "man hideth not." Perhaps we reveal ourselves too much in small things because we have so little of the great to conceal. The tiny incidents of daily routine are as much a commentary of racial ideals as the highest flight of philosophy or poetry. Even as the difference in favourite vintage marks the separate idiosyncrasies of different periods and nationalities of Europe, so the Tea-ideals characterise the various moods of Oriental culture. The **Cake-tea** which was boiled, the **Powdered-tea** which was whipped, the **Leaf-tea** which was steeped, mark the distinct emotional impulses of the Tang, the Sung, and the Ming dynasties of China. If we were inclined to borrow the much-abused terminology of art classification, we might designate them respectively, the **Classic**, the **Romantic**, and the **Naturalistic** schools of Tea.

The tea plant, a native of southern China, was known from very early times to Chinese botany and medicine. It is alluded to in the classics under the various names of Tou, Tseh, Chung, Kha, and Ming, and was highly prized for possessing the virtues of relieving fatigue, delighting the soul, strengthening the will, and repairing the eyesight. It was not only administered as an internal dose, but often applied externally in form of paste to alleviate rheumatic pains. The Taoists claimed it as an important ingredient of the **elixir of immortality**. The Buddhists used it

していた。

　4世紀ないし5世紀までには、茶は揚子江流域の住民の間で愛好される飲み物となっていた。現在の「茶」という表意文字が生まれたのもこの頃であるが、これは明らかに「檟（た）」の字の俗字である。南朝の詩人たちは「流れる翡翠（ひすい）の泡」への熱烈な賛辞をその詩に詠んでいる。歴代の皇帝は特別な功労への褒美として、高官たちに珍しい茶葉を下賜（かし）することもあった。しかし、この時期の茶の飲み方はきわめて原始的であった。葉は蒸して臼（うす）ですり潰し、団子にして、米、生姜、塩、蜜柑の皮、香料、牛乳、そしてときには玉葱まで入れて一緒に煮るのであった。この風習は今日でもチベットやモンゴルの諸部族の間に残っていて、彼らはこれらの混ぜ物から珍妙なシロップを作って飲んでいる。中国の隊商宿で茶を知ったロシア人がレモンの薄切りを用いるのは、この古くからの茶の淹れ方の名残である。

　茶がその未熟な段階から脱して、究極の理想に達するまでには、唐朝の時代精神が必要であった。8世紀中ごろの人物である陸羽によって初めて茶の伝道がはじまった。陸羽は仏教、道教、儒教が統合の道を模索していた時代に生まれた。その時代には、**汎神論的象徴主義**によって、個々の事物のなかに普遍的なものを見いだそうとする風潮が高まっていた。それゆえ詩人であ

▶陸羽
　733–804、唐の文筆家、茶の知識をまとめた『茶経（りくう）』の著者。

extensively to prevent drowsiness during their long hours of meditation.

By the fourth and fifth centuries Tea became a favourite beverage among the inhabitants of the Yang-tse-Kiang valley. It was about this time that the modern ideograph Cha was coined, evidently a corruption of the classic Tou. The poets of the southern dynasties have left some fragments of their fervent adoration of the "froth of the liquid jade." Then emperors used to bestow some rare preparation of the leaves on their high ministers as a reward for eminent services. Yet the method of drinking tea at this stage was primitive in the extreme. The leaves were steamed, crushed in a mortar, made into a cake, and boiled together with rice, ginger, salt, orange peel, spices, milk, and sometimes with onions! The custom obtains at the present day among the Thibetans and various Mongolian tribes, who make a curious syrup of these ingredients. The use of lemon slices by the Russians, who learned to take tea from the Chinese caravansaries, points to the survival of the ancient method.

It needed the genius of the Tang dynasty to emancipate Tea from its crude state and lead to its final idealisation. With Luwuh in the middle of the eighth century we have our first apostle of tea. He was born in an age when Buddhism, Taoism, and Confucian-ism were seeking mutual synthesis. The **pantheistic symbolism** of the time was urging one to mirror the Universal in the Particular. Luwuh, a poet, saw in

る陸羽は、**茶のもてなし**のうちにすべてのもの
を支配する調和と秩序を見いだしたのである。
彼の名高い著書である『茶経』（茶の聖典の意）
において、陸羽は「茶のとりきめ」を定式化した。
それ以来、彼は中国の茶商の守護神として崇め
られている。

　『茶経』は全3巻、10章から成っている。陸羽
は第1章で茶の木の性質について、第2章では
茶摘みの道具について、第3章では茶葉の選別
について述べている。それによれば、最良の茶葉

は、「韃靼人の騎手の皮靴のような皺がよってい
て、野牛の喉袋のように丸まり、峡谷に立つ霧の
ように広がり、そよ風の吹きわたる湖面のように
輝き、濡れれば雨で洗われた肥沃な大地のよう
に柔らかくならなくてはいけない」とのことで
ある。

　第4章は全24種の茶道具一式の列挙とその

説明に費やされていて、風炉に始まり、道具すべ
てを収納する竹製の茶篝筒に終わっている。こ
こでは陸羽に**道教的な象徴主義**への偏向がある
ことに気づかされる。ここで、茶が中国陶芸に及
ぼした影響について考察するのも興味深いこと
である。中国磁器は、周知の通り、翡翠の微妙な
色合いを再現しようとする試みに源を発してい
る。その結果、唐代に入ると、南方の**青磁**と北方
の**白磁**に分かれて生産されるようになった。陸
羽は青磁の茶碗を理想の色合いとした。青磁が
茶の緑の色合いを強めるのに対して、白磁は茶
に薄赤い色を与えて、まずそうにみせるからと

the **Tea-service** the same harmony and order which reigned through all things. In his celebrated work, the "Chaking" (*The Holy Scripture of Tea*) he formulated the Code of Tea. He has since been worshipped as the tutelary god of the Chinese tea merchants.

The "Chaking" consists of three volumes and ten chapters. In the first chapter Luwuh treats of the nature of the tea plant, in the second of the implements for gathering the leaves, in the third of the selection of the leaves. According to him the best quality of the leaves must have "creases like the leathern boot of Tartar horsemen, curl like the dew-lap of a mighty bullock, unfold like a mist rising out of a ravine, gleam like a lake touched by a zephyr, and be wet and soft like fine earth newly swept by rain."

The fourth chapter is devoted to the enumeration and description of the twenty-four members of the tea-equipage, beginning with the tripod brazier and ending with the bamboo cabinet for containing all these utensils. Here we notice Luwuh's predilection for **Taoist symbolism**. Also it is interesting to observe in this connection the influence of tea on Chinese ceramics. The Celestial porcelain, as is well known, had its origin in an attempt to reproduce the exquisite shade of jade, resulting, in the Tang dynasty, in the **blue glaze** of the south, and the **white glaze** of the north. Luwuh considered the blue as the ideal colour for the tea-cup, as it lent additional greenness to the

いう。これは陸羽が団茶を用いたためである。のちに宋の茶人が抹茶を用いるようになってからは、濃藍色や黒褐色の重い茶碗が好まれた。さらに明の時代になると、煎茶が用いられたので、軽い白磁の茶碗が好まれるようになったのである。

　第5章で陸羽は、茶の点て方について述べている。塩以外の混ぜ物は排除された。陸羽はまた、水の選定と、その沸かし加減についても詳述している。それによれば、山の湧き水が最高であり、つぎに川の水、井戸水はその次とされている。煮沸は3つの段階に分けられる。第1は魚の眼のような細かい泡が水面に浮かんだ段階、第2は泡が水晶の綴り玉のように連なって沸いてくる段階、第3は釜のなかで湯が激しく波立つ段階である。団茶は赤ん坊の腕のように柔らかくなるまで火で焙り、上質の紙に挟み、細かくほぐして粉とする。第1の沸き加減のところで塩を入れ、次の沸きで茶を入れる。さらに沸いたところでひとすくいの冷水を釜に入れて「**水の精気**」を蘇らせるのである。こうしてから茶碗に注いで飲む。その味わいやいかに！　透けるように薄い葉片は澄んだ空に漂ううろこ雲のようであり、翠玉色の流れに浮かぶ睡蓮のようでもある。唐の詩人盧同（ろどう）が詠ったのは、このような飲み物のことだったのだろう。「1杯飲めば、唇と喉が潤う。2杯飲めば、寂しさが癒やされる。3杯飲めば、枯れ果てた私の心に、5千巻もの奇妙な文字が浮かんでくる。4杯飲めば、軽く汗をかき、毛穴

▶盧同の茶歌
　親しい友人から贈られた新茶への感激を表した詩。

beverage, whereas the white made it look pinkish and distasteful. It was because he used cake-tea. Later on, when the tea-masters of Sung took to the powdered tea, they preferred heavy bowls of blue-black and dark brown. The Mings, with their steeped tea, rejoiced in light ware of white porcelain.

In the fifth chapter Luwuh describes the method of making tea. He eliminates all ingredients except salt. He dwells also on the much-discussed question of the choice of water and the degree of boiling it. According to him, the mountain spring is the best, the river water and the spring water come next in the order of excellence. There are three stages of boiling: the first boil is when the little bubbles like the eye of fishes swim on the surface; the second boil is when the bubbles are like crystal beads rolling in a fountain; the third boil is when the billows surge wildly in the kettle. The Cake-tea is roasted before the fire until it becomes soft like a baby's arm and is shredded into powder between pieces of fine paper. Salt is put in the first boil, the tea in the second. At the third boil, a dipperful of cold water is poured into the kettle to settle the tea and revive the "**youth of the water**." Then the beverage was poured into cups and drunk. O nectar! The filmy leaflet hung like scaly clouds in a serene sky or floated like water lilies on emerald streams. It was of such a beverage that Lotung, a Tang poet, wrote: "The first cup moistens my lips and throat, the second cup breaks my loneliness, the third cup searches my

から日頃の好ましからざるものがすべて抜けていく。5杯飲めば、この身は清浄無垢となる。6杯飲めば、**不老不死の国**に分け入ったかのようだ。7杯飲めば——ああ、もう何もいらない！ただ涼やかな風が袖を吹き抜けるのを感ずる。蓬莱山はどこにあるのか？　この爽やかな風に乗って、その地へ飛んで行きたい」

▶蓬莱山
　中国で仙人が住むといわれる山。

『茶経』の残りの章は、一般におこなわれている喫茶法の低俗さ、高名な茶人に関する史実、中国における有名な茶園、さまざまな茶のもてなし方、挿絵による**茶道具**の紹介などに費やされている。最後の章は惜しくも失われている。

『茶経』は世に出た当時には、かなりの評判を取ったと考えられる。陸羽は代宗帝（763～779）の後援を受け、その名声のもとに多くの門弟が集まった。**通人**のなかには、陸羽が点てた茶と、その弟子が点てた茶を見分けることができた者がいたといわれている。ある高官は、この名人の点てた茶の味がわからなかったため、不名誉にもその名を後世に遺したとされている。

宋代になると、抹茶が流行し、これが茶の第2の流れとなった。茶葉を小型の石臼で挽いてきめ細かな粉とし、竹を裂いて作った繊細な茶筅を使って、湯のなかで泡立てるのである。この新たな方法は、陸羽の茶道具にも、また葉の選定にも若干の変化をもたらした。これ以降、塩はまっ

barren entrail but to find therein some five thousand volumes of odd ideographs. The fourth cup raises a slight perspiration,—all the wrong of life passes away through my pores. At the fifth cup I am purified; the sixth cup calls me to the **realms of immortals**. The seventh cup—ah, but I could take no more! I only feel the breath of cool wind that rises in my sleeves. Where is Horaisan? Let me ride on this sweet breeze and waft away thither."

The remaining chapters of the "Chaking" treat of the vulgarity of the ordinary methods of tea-drinking, a historical summary of illustrious tea-drinkers, the famous tea plantations of China, the possible variations of the tea-service, and illustrations of the **tea-utensils**. The last is unfortunately lost.

The appearance of the "Chaking" must have created considerable sensation at the time. Luwuh was befriended by the Emperor Taisung (763–779), and his fame attracted many followers. Some **exquisites** were said to have been able to detect the tea made by Luwuh from that of his disciples. One mandarin has his name immortalised by his failure to appreciate the tea of this great master.

In the Sung dynasty the whipped tea came into fashion and created the second school of Tea. The leaves were ground to fine powder in a small stone mill, and the preparation was whipped in hot water by a delicate whisk made of split bamboo. The new process led to some change in the teaequipage of Luwuh, as well as

たく使われなくなった。宋の人々の茶への熱狂ぶりはとどまるところをしらなかった。**美食家**は競って新しい茶を求め、その優劣を決めるために定期的に競技会まで催された。名君というよりは偉大な芸術家であった徽宗帝（きそう）（1101～1124）は、珍しい茶葉を求めてその財を惜しまずに費やした。王自身20種の茶に関する論文を書いているが、そのなかでは「白茶」をもっとも珍重かつ高級な茶であるとしている。

　宋の人々の茶に対する理想は、その人生観が異なるように、唐の人々とは異なっていた。宋の人々は、先人が象徴化しようとしたものを現実化する道を模索した。**新儒教**の精神では、宇宙の法則は現象世界に映し出されているのではなく、現象世界が宇宙の法則そのものであるとしている。永劫（えいごう）とはただ瞬時の集合である——涅槃は常に手の届くところにある。不滅は永遠の変化のうちに存在すると考える道教の概念が、道家のあらゆる思考形態に浸透していた。人の興味を引くのは行為の過程であって、行為それ自体ではない。真に重要なのは完成への過程であって、完成されたもの自体ではないのである。人間はこのようにして自然と直面するに至った。人生に新しい意味合いが育まれるようになって、茶は風流な気晴らしにとどまらず、自己実現のひとつの方法となり始めたのである。王禹偁（おううしょう）は茶を賛美して「人の心に直に訴えかけてきて、その繊細な苦味は優れた助言の余韻を思わせる」

▶涅槃
　仏教における理想の境地。煩悩を断じた静寂の状態。

▶道家
　道教を信じる人。

the choice of leaves. Salt was discarded forever. The enthusiasm of the Sung people for tea knew no bounds. **Epicures** vied with each other in discovering new varieties, and regular tournaments were held to decide their superiority. The Emperor Kiasung (1101–1124), who was too great an artist to be a well-behaved monarch, lavished his treasures on the attainment of rare species. He himself wrote a dissertation on the twenty kinds of tea, among which he prizes the "white tea" as of the rarest and finest quality.

The tea-ideal of the Sungs differed from the Tangs even as their notion of life differed. They sought to actualise what their predecessors tried to symbolise. To the **Neo-Confucian** mind the cosmic law was not reflected in the phenomenal world, but the phenomenal world was the cosmic law itself. Æons were but moments—Nirvana always within grasp. The Taoist conception that immortality lay in the eternal change permeated all their modes of thought. It was the process, not the deed, which was interesting. It was the completing, not the completion, which was really vital. Man came thus at once face to face with nature. A new meaning grew into the art of life. The tea began to be not a poetical pastime, but one of the methods of self-realisation. Wangyu-cheng eulogised tea as "flooding his soul like a direct appeal, that its delicate bitterness reminded him of the aftertaste of a good counsel." Sotumpa wrote of the strength of the **immaculate purity** in tea which defied corruption

**▶蘇東坡**
　1036–1101、本名
は蘇軾。中国北宋
の詩人、書家。

**▶菩提達磨**
　禅宗の始祖。南
インドバラモンの
生まれ。嵩山の少
林寺にて9年間座
禅をした。

と述べている。蘇東坡は、茶に含まれる**清浄無垢**な力は、真に徳の高い人のように堕落を拒むといっている。仏教徒のうちでは、道教の教義を多く受け入れていた南方の禅宗が、茶の儀式をこと細かく組み立てた。禅僧らは菩提達磨の像の前に集まって、まるで聖餐のような恭しい儀礼をもって、1個の茶碗から茶を飲んだ。この禅の儀式が、やがて15世紀の日本の茶の湯へと発展していく。

　不幸にも、13世紀のモンゴル族の突然の勃興に際して、元朝がその蛮行によって中国を征服、略奪したことで、宋代の文化所産はことごとく破壊された。15世紀半ばから**国家再興**を試みた明朝は内紛に悩まされ、17世紀になると中国は再び異民族である満州族の支配下に置かれた。作法も風習も様変わりし、昔日の面影は跡形もなくなった。抹茶は完全に忘れ去られた。明のある訓古学者などは、宋代の古典に言及されている茶筅の形が思い出せず途方に暮れていたというのだ。茶は今では、葉を茶碗に入れ、湯を注ぎ、浸して飲むものになった。西欧世界が古式ゆかしい茶の飲み方について無知なのは、ヨーロッパ人は**明朝の末期**になってようやく茶の存在を知ったという事実によって説明できるわけだ。

　後世の中国人にとって、茶は美味しい飲み物ではあるが、理想ではなかった。長年にわたる中

as a truly virtuous man. Among the Buddhists, the southern Zen sect, which incorporated so much of Taoist doctrines, formulated an elaborate ritual of tea. The monks gathered before the image of Bodhi Dharma and drank tea out of a single bowl with the profound formality of a holy sacrament. It was this Zen ritual which finally developed into the Tea-ceremony of Japan in the fifteenth century.

Unfortunately the sudden outburst of the Mongol tribes in the thirteenth century, which resulted in the devastation and conquest of China under the barbaric rule of the Yuen Emperors, destroyed all the fruits of Sung culture. The native dynasty of the Mings which attempted **re-nationalisation** in the middle of the fifteenth century was harassed by internal troubles, and China again fell under the alien rule of the Manchus in the seventeenth century. Manners and customs changed to leave no vestige of the former times. The powdered tea is entirely forgotten. We find a Ming commentator at loss to recall the shape of the tea whisk mentioned in one of the Sung classics. Tea is now taken by steeping the leaves in hot water in a bowl or cup. The reason why the Western world is innocent of the older method of drinking tea is explained by the fact that Europe knew it only at the **close of the Ming dynasty**.

To the latter-day Chinese tea is a delicious beverage, but not an ideal. The long woes of his country have

国の災禍は、中国人から人生の意義に対する強い興味を奪ってしまった。中国は近代化された。すなわち、時を経て幻滅を味わったのである。彼らは詩人や古人が永遠の若さと活力の源としていた幻想への気高い信念を失ってしまった。**折衷主義**を奉じるようになり、世界の慣わしを従順に受け入れるばかりだ。自然を弄びはするが、へりくだって、征服したり、崇拝したりはしない。彼らの茶葉は花のような香りのする妙なるものだが、その茶碗からは唐や宋代の儀式にみられたロマンスは失われてしまったのだ。

　中国文明の足跡をそのままたどってきた日本は、茶の３つの段階をすべて知ることになった。すでに729年に、聖武天皇が奈良の宮廷で百人の僧侶に茶をふるまったと記録されている。茶葉はおそらく**遣唐使**によってもたらされ、その時代の風習に従って淹れられたのだろう。801年には僧最澄が茶の種を持ち帰り、比叡山に植えている。それに続く数世紀にわたって多くの茶園が造られたことが知られており、茶は貴族や僧侶が好む飲み物となった。宋の茶は1191年、南方禅の流派に学んでいた栄西禅師の帰国とともに日本に伝来した。禅師が持ち帰った新しい種は３ヵ所に植えられ、そのうちの１ヵ所である京都近郊の宇治は、今日まで、世界最高の茶の産地として知られている。南方禅は驚くほどの速さで広まり、それにともなって宋の茶の儀式と茶の理想も伝わった。15世紀の将軍足利義政の時代までには、茶の湯は完成をみて、独立

▶**最澄**
　767-822、天台宗の開祖。

▶**栄西**
　1141-1215、臨済宗の開祖。宋から茶種を持ち帰り、『喫茶養生記』を著す。

▶**南方禅**
　中国禅のうち、北方禅が段階的な悟りを説くのに対し、突然の悟りを説くとする派。南方に勢力があった。

robbed him of the zest for the meaning of life. He has become modern, that is to say, old and disenchanted. He has lost that sublime faith in illusions which constitutes the eternal youth and vigour of the poets and ancients. He is an **eclectic** and politely accepts the traditions of the universe. He toys with Nature, but does not condescend to conquer or worship her. His Leaf-tea is often wonderful with its flower-like aroma, but the romance of the Tang and Sung ceremonials are not to be found in his cup.

Japan, which followed closely on the footsteps of Chinese civilisation, has known the tea in all its three stages. As early as the year 729 we read of the Emperor Shomu giving tea to one hundred monks at his palace in Nara. The leaves were probably imported by our **ambassadors to the Tang Court** and prepared in the way then in fashion. In 801 the monk Saicho brought back some seeds and planted them in Yeisan. Many tea-gardens are heard of in the succeeding centuries, as well as the delight of the aristocracy and priesthood in the beverage. The Sung tea reached us in 1191 with the return of Yeisai-zenji, who went there to study the southern Zen school. The new seeds which he carried home were successfully planted in three places, one of which, the Uji district near Kioto, bears still the name of producing the best tea in the world. The southern Zen spread with marvellous rapidity, and with it the tea-ritual and the tea-ideal of the Sung.

した現世のひとつの芸道となっていた。それ以来、茶道は日本において完全に確立されたのである。のちに中国で用いられるようになった煎茶は、日本でも知られ、17世紀半ば以降に飲まれるようになったのだから比較的最近といっていい。普段の消費においては煎茶が抹茶にとって代わったが、抹茶はいまだに茶のなかの茶としてその地位を保ち続けている。

われわれが茶の理想の極致をみるのは、日本の茶の湯の儀式においてである。1281年の**蒙古襲来**を阻止したことで日本は、中国では遊牧民族の侵略によって不幸にも中断された宋の文化を継続することができた。日本人にとっての茶は、喫茶法を単に理想化するものではなく、**生の術を教えてくれる宗教**なのである。茶という飲料は純粋と洗練の崇拝のための口実——すなわち主人と客が一体となって、この世の無上のよろこびを創り出すという神聖な役割を果たすまでに成長したのである。茶室はこの世という寂しい荒野のオアシスである。そこで疲れた旅人は、芸術享受という共通の泉で渇きを癒やすことができる。茶の湯は、茶と花と絵画が織りなす即興劇である。茶室の雰囲気を損なう色はひとつとしてなく、その韻律を破る響きも、調和を乱す動きもなく、周辺世界の均一をみだす言葉もない。すべての動作は単純で自然におこなわれる——それこそが茶の湯の目標なのであるから。そして不思議なことではあるが、これはおうお

By the fifteenth Yoshimasa, the tea-ceremony is fully constituted and made into an independent and secular performance. Since then Teaism is fully established in Japan. The use of the steeped tea of the later China is comparatively recent among us, being only known since the middle of the seventeenth century. It has replaced the Powdered-tea in ordinary consumption, though the latter still continues to hold its place as the tea of teas.

It is in the Japanese tea-ceremony that we see the culmination of tea-ideals. Our successful resistance of the **Mongol invasion** in 1281 had enabled us to carry on the Sung movement so disastrously cut off in China itself through the nomadic inroad. Tea with us became more than an idealisation of the form of drinking; it is a **religion of the art of life**. The beverage grew to be an excuse for the worship of purity and refinement, a sacred function at which the host and guest joined to produce for that occasion the utmost beatitude of the mundane. The tea-room was an oasis in the dreary waste of existence where weary travellers could meet to drink from the common spring of art-appreciation. The ceremony was an improvised drama whose plot was woven about the tea, the flowers, and the paintings. Not a colour to disturb the tone of the room, not a sound to mar the rhythm of things, not a gesture to obtrude on the harmony, not a word to break the unity of the surroundings, all movements to be performed simply and naturally—such were the aims of the tea-ceremony.

うにして成功している。その背後には精妙な哲
理が存在する。茶道は姿を変えた道家思想とも
いえるのである。

And strangely enough it was often successful. A subtle philosophy lay behind it all. Teaism was Taoism in disguise.

# 第 3 章　道教と禅

## Chapter 3　Taoism and Zennism

▶老子
　春秋戦国時代
（前770–前221）の
思想家、道家の祖。

▶函谷関
　中国河南省北西
部にある有名な関
所。

　禅と茶のつながりはよく知られている。茶道
が禅の儀式を発展させたものであることは先に
述べたが、道教の祖である老子の名も茶の歴史
と密接な関係にある。習慣や風習の起源を記し
た中国の教科書には、客に茶を供する礼法は、老
子の門弟である関尹が函谷関で、「老哲人」に金
色の仙薬をささげたことに始まると書いてある。
そんなに古くから道家の徒のあいだではこの飲
料が用いられていたのだろうかと、真偽のほど
を議論してみることも価値あることではあるが、
それよりもわれわれがここで興味を覚えるのは、
茶道のなかに具体化されている人生と芸術につ
いての道教と禅の思想である。

　道教と禅の教えについては外国語でも紹介し
ようといろいろと手は尽くされてきたようだが、
残念ながらまだ十分なものはあらわれていない。

　翻訳にはいつも裏切られてばかりだ。明代の
ある作家もこう言っている。うまくいったとして
も錦の裏側を見せられるだけで、そこに縦横の
糸はあっても色彩や意匠の精緻はわからないと。
だが、容易に説明できる**大教義**など存在するの

The connection of **Zennism** with tea is proverbial. We have already remarked that the tea-ceremony was a development of the Zen ritual. The name of Laotse, the founder of Taoism, is also intimately associated with the history of tea. It is written in the Chinese school manual concerning the origin of habits and customs that the ceremony of offering tea to a guest began with Kwanyin, a well-known disciple of Laotse, who first at the gate of the Han Pass presented to the "Old Philosopher" a cup of the golden elixir. We shall not stop to discuss the authenticity of such tales, which are valuable, however, as confirming the early use of the beverage by the Taoists. Our interest in Taoism and Zennism here lies mainly in those ideas regarding life and art which are so embodied in what we call Teaism.

It is to be regretted that as yet there appears to be no adequate presentation of the Taoist and Zen doctrines in any foreign language, though we have had several laudable attempts.

Translation is always a treason, and as a Ming author observes, can at its best be only the reverse side of a brocade,—all the threads are there, but not the subtlety of colour or design. But, after all, what **great doctrine** is there which is easy to expound? The **ancient**

だろうか。**古の賢人**も自らの教えを系統立てて説こうとはしなかった。彼らが逆説をもって説いたのは、真理の反面だけを伝えてしまうことを危惧したからである。語りはじめは愚者のようであっても、終わるころには聞くものを賢ならしめる。老子みずからも巧みなユーモアを込めてこう言っている。「教養の低い者に**道**を説けば大笑いされる。もし笑われなければそれは道ではない」

「道」とは、直訳すれば「経路」を意味する。それは、「行路」、「絶対」、「法則」、「自然」、「至理」、「方式」と訳されたりもする。どれも誤りではない。なぜなら問われた内容により道教の徒は使い分けるからである。このことについて、老子みずからこう語っている。「物有り混成し、天地に先立って生ず。寂たり寥たり。独立して改めず。周行してあやうからず。もって天下の母となすべし。われその名を知らず。これを字して道という。強いてこれが名をなして大という。大を逝といい、逝を遠といい、遠を反という」「道」は「経路」に、というより「移りゆく経過」にある。**宇宙変遷**の精神、すなわち新しい形を生み出そうとして自らに戻り、永遠に成長する。「道」は道教の象徴である龍のごとくはね返り、雲のように巻いては解かれていく。「道」は**大いなる推移**であるといっていい。主観的にとらえれば宇宙の気。その絶対は相対的なものなのだ。


まずはじめに記憶すべきことは、道教はその

**sages** never put their teachings in systematic form. They spoke in paradoxes, for they were afraid of uttering half-truths. They began by talking like fools and ended by making their hearers wise. Laotse himself, with his quaint humour, says, "If people of inferior intelligence hear of the **Tao**, they laugh immensely. It would not be the Tao unless they laughed at it."

The Tao literally means a Path. It has been severally translated as the Way, the Absolute, the Law, Nature, Supreme Reason, the Mode. These renderings are not incorrect, for the use of the term by the Taoists differs according to the subject-matter of the inquiry. Laotse himself spoke of it thus: "There is a thing which is all-containing, which was born before the existence of Heaven and Earth. How silent! How solitary! It stands alone and changes not. It revolves without danger to itself and is the mother of the universe. I do not know its name and so call it the Path. With reluctance I call it the Infinite. Infinity is the Fleeting, the Fleeting is the Vanishing, the Vanishing is the Reverting." The Tao is in the Passage rather than the Path. It is the spirit of **Cosmic Change**,—the eternal growth which returns upon itself to produce new forms. It recoils upon itself like the dragon, the beloved symbol of the Taoists. It folds and unfolds as do the clouds. The Tao might be spoken of as the **Great Transition**. Subjectively it is the Mood of the Universe. Its Absolute is the Relative.

It should be remembered in the first place that

流れを正統に受け継ぐ禅と同じく南方中国の個人主義的傾向をあらわしており、これは儒教にみられる北方中国の社会主義的体制とは対比をなしているということだ。ヨーロッパ全域と同じくらい広大な**中国**は、ふたつの大河によって分かたれ、それぞれ土地固有の特質を持っている。**揚子江**と**黄河**は、地中海やバルト海にあたる。統一後、幾世紀を経た今日でも南方と北方とで思想や信仰が異なっているのは、ラテン民族とチュートン民族とが異なっているのと同様である。互いに行き来することが今日よりいっそう困難だった時代、とくに封建時代において思想の相違はもっと明確であった。芸術、詩歌にあらわれる雰囲気もまるで異なるのだ。老子とその徒、そして揚子江沿いの自然詩人の先駆けである屈原らが抱いていた理想主義は、同時代の北方の作家たちのつまらぬ道徳観念とはまったく相容れないものだった。老子が生きていた紀元前5世紀ごろのことである。

▶**チュートン人**
　古代ゲルマン族の一派、もしくはドイツ、オランダなどの北欧民族。

▶**屈原**
　前343-前277頃、戦国時代の詩人、文筆家。

　道教思想の萌芽は、老聃と字された老子の出現よりずっと以前にみられる。古代中国の記録、とくに『易経』は老子の思想の徴候を示している。しかし紀元前12世紀、周王朝の確立とともに頂点を極めた古代中国文明社会では法律や風習が重要視されたため、個人思想は長い間その発展を阻まれてきた。そのため周王朝が崩壊し

▶**易経**
　儒教の基本五経の経典のひとつ。

Taoism, like its legitimate successor, Zennism, represents the individualistic trend of the Southern Chinese mind in contradistinction to the communism of Northern China which expressed itself in Confucianism. The **Middle Kingdom** is as vast as Europe and has a differentiation of idiosyncrasies marked by the two great river systems which traverse it. The **Yangtse-Kiang** and **Hoang-Ho** are respectively the Mediterranean and the Baltic. Even today, in spite of centuries of unification, the Southern Celestial differs in his thoughts and beliefs from his Northern brother as a member of the Latin race differs from the Teuton. In ancient days, when communication was even more difficult than at present, and especially during the feudal period, this difference in thought was most pronounced. The art and poetry of the one breathes an atmosphere entirely distinct from that of the other. In Laotse and his followers and in Kutsugen, the forerunner of the Yangtse-Kiang nature-poets, we find an idealism quite inconsistent with the prosaic ethical notions of their contemporary northern writers. Laotse lived five centuries before the Christian Era.

The germ of Taoist speculation may be found long before the advent of Laotse, surnamed the Long-Eared. The archaic records of China, especially the **Book of Changes**, foreshadow his thought. But the great respect paid to the laws and customs of that classic period of Chinese civilisation which culminated with the establishment of the Chow dynasty in the twelfth

てあまたの独立国家が誕生するにおよんで、自由思想の豊かな花を咲かせることができたのである。老子と荘子はともに南方の出身で、新思潮の提唱者だった。一方、孔子は多くの門弟とともに古来の伝統を保持しようと志した。道教を理解するためには儒教の知識もある程度は必要で、この逆もまた然りである。

▶荘子
前369-前286年頃、老子と並び称される道教の始祖の一人。

▶孔子
前551-前479年頃、春秋時代の思想家。儒家の始祖。

　道教における**絶対**は**相対的**であるということはすでに述べた。倫理において道教の徒たちは社会の法律や道徳を罵倒した。なぜなら彼らにとって善と悪は相対的な言葉に過ぎないからだ。定義することは制限することであり、「一定」とか「不変」といった言葉は成長の停止をあらわすことになる。屈原いわく「賢人は世とともに推移する」。われわれの道徳規範は過去の社会の必要から生まれたものだが、社会は常に同じであろうか？　共同社会の伝統を守るためには、国家に対する個人の犠牲を免れない。教育とは、強大な思い込みを続けさせるために一種の無知を奨励するものだ。真に高潔な人物になるためではなく、**行儀よくふるまう**ために教えられるのである。われわれは恐ろしく自意識が強いため不道徳をおこなう。自分自身が悪いと知っているから他人を許すことができない。他人に真実を語ってしまうことを恐れるがゆえに良心を

century b.c., kept the development of individualism in check for a long while, so that it was not until after the disintegration of the Chow dynasty and the establishment of innumerable independent kingdoms that it was able to blossom forth in the luxuriance of free-thought. Laotse and Soshi (Chuangtse) were both Southerners and the greatest exponents of the New School. On the other hand Confucius with his numerous disciples aimed at retaining ancestral conventions. Taoism cannot be understood without some knowledge of Confucianism and vice versa.

We have said that the Taoist **Absolute** was the **Relative**. In ethics the Taoist railed at the laws and the moral codes of society, for to them right and wrong were but relative terms. Definition is always limitation—the "fixed" and "unchangeless" are but terms expressive of a stoppage of growth. Said Kutsugen, "The Sages move the world." Our standards of morality are begotten of the past needs of society, but is society to remain always the same? The observance of communal traditions involves a constant sacrifice of the individual to the state. Education, in order to keep up the mighty delusion, encourages a species of ignorance. People are not taught to be really virtuous, but to **behave properly**. We are wicked because we are frightfully self-conscious. We never forgive others because we know that we ourselves are in the wrong. We nurse a conscience because we are afraid to tell the truth to others; we take refuge in pride because we are afraid to tell the

抱き、自分に真実を語ってしまうことを恐れるがゆえに自尊心へ逃げ込む。世の中自体がばかげているのにどうしてまじめでいられよう！

**物々交換**の精神はどこにでもあるではないか。名誉だ貞節だ！と言いながらも、善と真実を小売りして悦に入った売り子をみよ。いわゆる宗教さえも買うことができるのだ。だがそれはありふれた道徳を花と音楽で清めたものにすぎない。教会からこうした装飾物を取り去ると、あとに何が残るだろうか？　にもかかわらず宗教市場はすばらしく繁盛している。どれも話にならないほど値段が安いからである。天国行きの切符を手に入れるための祈祷（きとう）、名誉市民となるための公文書——いますぐに身を隠すがよい。おのれが有益な人物であると世に知れたなら、すぐに**競売**にかけられて最高額入札者に落札されてしまうことになるだろう。男も女もそれほどなぜ自分自身を宣伝したがるのだろうか？　奴隷制度からの本能にすぎないのだろうか？

　力強い思想というものは、同時代の思想を打ち破り、そしてその後に続いて起きたさまざまな動きを支配したことからもうかがえる。秦——中国を統一した王朝で、チャイナという名前もこれに由来する——の時代、道教は一大勢力であった。もし時間の余裕があれば、道教がその時代の思想家、数学者、兵法家、神秘主義者、錬金術師、それにのちの揚子江派自然詩人らに及ぼした影響に注目してみるのもいいだろう。白馬は白いから実在するのか、もしくは固いから実

▶秦
　春秋戦国時代の大国。前221年に天下を統一した。

truth to ourselves. How can one be serious with the world when the world itself is so ridiculous! The spirit of **barter** is everywhere. Honour and Chastity! Behold the complacent salesman retailing the Good and True. One can even buy a so-called Religion, which is really but common morality sanctified with flowers and music. Rob the Church of her accessories and what remains behind? Yet the trusts thrive marvelously, for the prices are absurdly cheap,—a prayer for a ticket to heaven, a diploma for an honourable citizenship. Hide yourself under a bushel quickly, for if your real usefulness were known to the world you would soon be knocked down to the highest bidder by the **public auctioneer**. Why do men and women like to advertise themselves so much? Is it not but an instinct derived from the days of slavery?

The virility of the idea lies not less in its power of breaking through contemporary thought than in its capacity for dominating subsequent movements. Taoism was an active power during the Shin dynasty, that epoch of Chinese unification from which we derive the name of China. It would be interesting had we time to note its influence on contemporary thinkers, the mathematicians, writers on law and war, the mystics and alchemists and the later nature-poets of the Yangtse-Kiang. We should not even ignore those

▶六朝時代
222-589年、三国
時代の呉、東晋、南
朝の宋、斉、梁、陳
をあわせた時代。

▶清談家
芸術、学問など
について話す人。

▶列子
春秋戦国時代の
道家のひとり。寓
話を多く残してい
る。

在するのかと疑った**実在論者**や、禅の哲学者のように「純粋」と「絶対」について議論しあった六朝時代の清談家も無視することはできないだろう。とりわけ道教が**中国の国民性**の形成に寄与し、「翡翠のような温かみ」とも例えられる慎み深さと上品さをもたらした点については敬意を払うべきである。中国の歴史には、道教の信者たちが王侯も隠者もみなその教義を従おうとした結果生まれた興味深い話がいくつも残されている。その話には教訓や楽しみが必ずある。**逸話、寓話、警句**もふんだんにある。生きていたことがないから死ぬこともないという愉快な皇帝と、言葉を交わせるくらいの間柄になってみたいものだ。列子とともに風に乗り、絶対の静寂を味わうこともできるだろう。なぜならわたしたち自身が風なのだから。または、天にも属さず地にも属さぬゆえに、その中間に住むという黄河の老人とともに中空にとどまろうか。このように、現在の中国では奇怪で名ばかりとなってしまった道教のなかにさえ、ほかの新興宗教にはみられないようなたくさんの比喩話を楽しむことができるのである。

　しかし道教がアジアの生活にもたらした主な貢献は、美学の領域にある。中国の歴史家は道教のことを「**処世術**」と常にいっている。というのも、道教は現在を——われら自身のことを扱っているからである。神と自然が出会うところも、

speculators on Reality who doubted whether a white horse was real because he was white, or because he was solid, nor the Conversationalists of the Six dynasties who, like the Zen philosophers, revelled in discussions concerning the Pure and the Abstract. Above all we should pay homage to Taoism for what it has done toward the formation of the **Celestial character**, giving to it a certain capacity for reserve and refinement as "warm as jade." Chinese history is full of instances in which the votaries of Taoism, princes and hermits alike, followed with varied and interesting results the teachings of their creed. The tale will not be without its quota of instruction and amusement. It will be rich in **anecdotes, allegories,** and **aphorisms**. We would fain be on speaking terms with the delightful emperor who never died because he never lived. We may ride the wind with Liehtse and find it absolutely quiet because we ourselves are the wind, or dwell in mid-air with the Aged One of the Hoang-Ho, who lived betwixt Heaven and Earth because he was subject to neither the one nor the other. Even in that grotesque apology for Taoism which we find in China at the present day, we can revel in a wealth of imagery impossible to find in any other cult.

But the chief contribution of Taoism to Asiatic life has been in the realm of æsthetics. Chinese historians have always spoken of Taoism as the "**art of being in the world**," for it deals with the present—ourselves. It is in us that God meets with Nature, and yesterday parts

昨日が明日と分かれるところもわれらのうちにある。「現在」とは**移動する「無限」**であり、「相対」の正当な活動範囲である。「相対性」は「**調整**」を求める。「調整」とは「術」である。この世に生きる術はわれらを取り巻く環境を調整し続けるところにある。道教はこの世をありのままに受け入れ、儒教徒や仏教徒とは異なり、悲しみや苦しみの世の中に美を見出そうとするものだ。宋代の寓話に「酢を味わう3人」という、3つの教義それぞれを見事にあらわしている物語がある。酢がはいった甕——人生の象徴——のまわりに、釈迦牟尼、孔子、老子が立ち、それぞれ指先に酢につけて味わった。率直な孔子は酸っぱいといい、釈迦は苦いといい、老子は甘いと断言したというのである。

　道教徒はこういった。もしみなで全体のまとまりを保とうとすれば、人生劇はもっとおもしろくすることができると。ものごとの釣り合いを保ち、おのれの地歩を失うことなく他人に場所を譲ることが、この世の芝居で成功する秘訣なのだ。それぞれが自分の役を立派に勤め上げるためには、芝居全体を知らねばならない。個人のことを考えるなかで、全体を考えることを忘れてはいけないのだ。これを老子は「**虚**」というお得意の隠喩で説明している。彼は真に不可欠なものは虚にのみ存在すると言った。たとえば部屋の実体は、屋根と壁に囲まれた空虚な場所に見出されるのであって、屋根と壁それ自体にはない。水差しが役に立つのも水を注ぎいれるこ

from tomorrow. The Present is the **moving Infinity**, the legitimate sphere of the Relative. Relativity seeks **Adjustment**; Adjustment is Art. The art of life lies in a constant readjustment to our surroundings. Taoism accepts the mundane as it is and, unlike the Confucians and the Buddhists, tries to find beauty in our world of woe and worry. The Sung allegory of the Three Vinegar Tasters explains admirably the trend of the three doctrines. Sakyamuni, Confucius, and Laotse once stood before a jar of vinegar—the emblem of life—and each dipped in his fingers to taste the brew. The matter-of-fact Confucius found it sour, the Buddha called it bitter, and Laotse pronounced it sweet.

The Taoists claimed that the comedy of life could be made more interesting if everyone would preserve the unities. To keep the proportion of things and give place to others without losing one's own position was the secret of success in the mundane drama. We must know the whole play in order to properly act our parts; the conception of totality must never be lost in that of the individual. This Laotse illustrates by his favourite metaphor of the **Vacuum**. He claimed that only in vacuum lay the truly essential. The reality of a room, for instance, was to be found in the vacant space enclosed by the roof and walls, not in the roof and walls themselves. The usefulness of a water pitcher dwelt in the emptiness where water might be put, not in

とができる空間があるからであり、水差しの形や製品の素材にあるわけではない。虚はすべてを含むことができるので万能である。虚においてのみ運動が可能である。おのれを虚にして他を自由にむかえ入れることができる人は、あらゆる状況を支配できるだろう。全体が常に部分を支配できるのである。

道教徒のこういう考え方は、剣術や格闘技に至るまで、われわれの運動理論に非常な影響を与えてきた。日本の**護身術**である柔術は、その名を『道徳経』の一節からとっている。柔術では**無抵抗**、すなわち虚によって敵に力を出し尽くさせ、おのれの力は最後の戦いに備えて温存しておく。芸術においても、同じ原理の重要性が暗示の価値によって説明されている。何もいわないでおくところに、見る者は考えを完成させる機会を与えられる。それによって偉大な傑作は強烈に見る者の注意をひきつけ、自分も実際にその作品の一部になったかのように思わせる。そこにはあなたの美的感情を受け入れ、極限まで満たせるような虚があるのである。

生の術を身につけた者が、道教徒がいうところの「**真の人間**」である。真の人間は生まれるとともに夢の世界に入り、死に際して初めて現実に目を覚ます。真の人間は他の人間たちと自分をさりげなく同化させるために、自分の賢さを抑えるものだ。真の人間は「予として冬に川を渉るがごとく、猶として四隣を畏るるがごとく、儼として它れ客のごとく、渙として氷のまさ

▶『道徳経』
老子が著した道家の代表的書物。

the form of the pitcher or the material of which it was made. Vacuum is all potent because all containing. In vacuum alone motion becomes possible. One who could make of himself a vacuum into which others might freely enter would become master of all situations. The whole can always dominate the part.

These Taoists' ideas have greatly influenced all our theories of action, even to those of fencing and wrestling. Jiu-jitsu, the Japanese **art of self-defence**, owes its name to a passage in the **Taoteiking**. In jiu-jitsu one seeks to draw out and exhaust the enemy's strength by **non-resistance**, vacuum, while conserving one's own strength for victory in the final struggle. In art the importance of the same principle is illustrated by the value of suggestion. In leaving something unsaid the beholder is given a chance to complete the idea and thus a great masterpiece irresistibly rivets your attention until you seem to become actually a part of it. A vacuum is there for you to enter and fill up to the full measure of your æsthetic emotion.

He who had made himself master of the art of living was the **Real Man** of the Taoist. At birth he enters the realm of dreams only to awaken to reality at death. He tempers his own brightness in order to merge himself into the obscurity of others. He is "reluctant, as one who crosses a stream in winter; hesitating, as one who fears the neighbourhood; respectful, like a guest; trembling, like ice that is about to melt; unassuming,

に釈けんとするがごとく、敦としてそれ樸のごとく、曠としてそれ谷のごとく、混としてそれ濁れるがごとし」。真の人間にとっての人生の三宝は、**慈悲、倹約、謙譲**なのである。

さて、禅に注意を向けてみると、禅が道教の教えを強調しているのがわかる。禅は梵語の禅那に由来する名前で瞑想を意味する。ひたすら瞑想することで自己実現の極致に達するであろうと禅は主張しているのだ。瞑想は六波羅蜜のひとつであり、それを通して**悟りの境地**に至ることができるかもしれず、釈迦牟尼は晩年の教えにおいて特にこの方法に重きを置き、それらの規則を高弟の迦葉に伝えたと、禅宗徒は確信している。言い伝えによれば、禅の始祖である迦葉はその奥義を阿難陀に伝え、それは阿難陀から順に祖師に伝わっていき、第28祖菩提達磨にまで達した。菩提達磨は6世紀の初めに北方中国へ渡り、中国禅宗の開祖となった。祖師やその教義の歴史に関しては、不明な部分が多いが、哲学的な側面から見た初期の禅学は、一方では那伽閼刺樹那のインド否定論に似ており、他方では商羯羅阿闍利の組み立てた**無明観**に似ているように思われる。今日私たちが知っている禅の最初の教えは、南方禅——南方中国にその勢力があったことからそう呼ばれている——の開祖である第6祖慧能（637〜713）によるものである。慧能ののち、ほどなくして馬祖（〜788）が続き、禅は中国人の生活のなかに深く影響を及ぼすこととなった。馬祖の弟子、百丈

▶**六波羅蜜**
　【仏】6種の基本的な修行の項目。布施、持戒、忍辱、精神、禅定、智慧。

▶**高弟**
　後継者とされる人。

▶**祖師**
　【仏】開祖。宗派を開いた人。

▶**慧能**
　唐代の僧で、禅宗の大成者。

like a piece of wood not yet carved; vacant, like a valley; formless, like troubled waters." To him the three jewels of life were **Pity, Economy,** and **Modesty**.

If now we turn our attention to Zennism we shall find that it emphasises the teachings of Taoism. Zen is a name derived from the Sanscrit word Dhyana, which signifies meditation. It claims that through consecrated meditation may be attained supreme selfrealisation. Meditation is one of the six ways through which **Buddhahood** may be reached, and the Zen sectarians affirm that Sakyamuni laid special stress on this method in his later teachings, handing down the rules to his chief disciple Kashiapa. According to their tradition Kashiapa, the first Zen patriarch, imparted the secret to Ananda, who in turn passed it on to successive patriarchs until it reached Bodhi Dharma, the twenty-eighth. Bodhi Dharma came to Northern China in the early half of the sixth century and was the first patriarch of Chinese Zen. There is much uncertainty about the history of these patriarchs and their doctrines. In its philosophical aspect early Zennism seems to have affinity on one hand to the Indian Negativism of Nagarjuna and on the other to the **Gnan philosophy** formulated by Sanchara-charya. The first teaching of Zen as we know it at the present day must be attributed to the sixth Chinese patriarch Yeno (637–713), founder of Southern Zen, so-called from the fact of its predominance in Southern China. He is closely followed by the great Baso (died 788) who

▶禅林
　修行をする者た
ちが集まるところ
を林にたとえ、一
般に禅宗の寺院の
こと。

（719～814）は、初めて**禅林**を開設し、その儀
式や規則をまとめた。馬祖の時代以後の禅宗の
問答をみると、もとのインド理想主義とは対照
的な、揚子江河畔精神の影響を受けた中国固有
の考え方が広まっていることがみてとれる。い
かに宗派の誇りがそうではないと主張したとこ
ろで、中国禅宗が老子や道教の清談家たちの教
えに似ている印象は否めない。『道徳経』には、
精神集中の重要性や適切な呼吸法の必要性が述
べられている。これはまさに禅における瞑想の
実践に欠かせないものである。老子の教えに対
する注釈の何冊かは、禅学者によって書かれて
いるほどなのだ。

　禅道は道教と同じく相対を崇拝している。ある
禅師は禅を定義して南天に北極星を見る術であ
るとしている。真理は反対のものを理解すること
によってのみ達せられる。禅道はまた、道教と同
じく個人主義を強く提唱している。自分たちの精
神の働きに関係しないものはいっさい存在しな
いというのである。第6祖慧能は、二人の僧が風
にはためく仏塔の幡をみながら話しているのを
見た。「動いているのは風である」と一人が言う
と、「動いているのは幡である」ともう一人が言っ
た。しかし慧能は彼らにこう説いた。「動いてい
るのは風でも幡でもない。心の中の何かである」
百丈が弟子と森の中を歩いていると、野うさぎが

▶幡
【仏】法要の場を
飾り供養する旗。

made of Zen a living influence in Celestial life. Hiakujo (719–814), the pupil of Baso, first instituted the **Zen monastery** and established a ritual and regulations for its government. In the discussions of the Zen school after the time of Baso we find the play of the Yangtse Kiang mind causing an accession of native modes of thought in contrast to the former Indian idealism. Whatever sectarian pride may assert to the contrary, one cannot help being impressed by the similarity of Southern Zen to the teachings of Laotse, and the Taoist Conversationalists. In the Taoteiking we already find allusions to the importance of self-concentration and the need of properly regulating the breath—essential points in the practice of Zen meditation. Some of the best commentaries on the Book of Laotse have been written by Zen scholars.

Zennism, like Taoism, is the worship of Relativity. One master defines Zen as the art of feeling the polar star in the southern sky. Truth can be reached only through the comprehension of opposites. Again, Zennism, like Taoism, is a strong advocate of individualism. Nothing is real except that which concerns the working of our own minds. Yeno, the sixth patriarch, once saw two monks watching the flag of a pagoda fluttering in the wind. One said "It is the wind that moves," the other said "It is the flag that moves"; but Yeno explained to them that the real movement was neither of the wind nor the flag, but of something within their own minds. Hiakujo was walking in the forest with a disciple when

二人が近づいてくるのに気がついて走り去って
しまった。「なぜ野うさぎはお前から逃げたのだ
ろう？」と百丈が問いかけると、「私を恐れたの
でしょう」と答えた。「ちがう」と師は言った。「そ
れはお前のなかに残忍性があるからだ」 この対
話は道教の徒である荘子を思い起こさせる。あ
る日、荘子は友と川のほとりを歩いていた。「魚
たちはなんと楽しそうに泳いでいることか」と
荘子は声をあげると、友はこういった。「きみは
魚でもないのに、なぜ魚たちが楽しんでいるとわ
かるのか？」「きみは私ではないのに、魚たちが
楽しんでいることを私がわからないと、どうして
きみがわかるのだ」と荘子は答えたという。

　禅は、道教が儒教と相反したように、正統派
の仏教の教えとしばしば相反した。禅の本質を
徹底的に見抜こうとすれば、言葉は思想の妨げ
にしかならない。どんな**仏典**をもってしても、そ
れはただの個人的思索の注釈にすぎない。禅門
の徒は物事の内にある本質と直接に交感しよう
と志し、外面の付属物は真理を認知するために
はただの邪魔者とみなした。この「抽象」を愛
する精神こそが、禅門の徒に古典仏教派の精巧
な彩色画よりも墨絵の素描を選ばせるのである。
禅門の徒のなかには、偶像や象徴によらず自分
自身のなかの仏陀を認めようと努めた結果、**偶
像破壊主義者**となった者もいる。ある冬の日、丹
霞和尚が木仏を打ち壊して火を起こしたという
話がある。そばにいた者が非常に驚いて「なん
と罰当たりなことを！」と言った。「仏像を焼い

a hare scurried off at their approach. "Why does the hare fly from you?" asked Hiakujo. "Because he is afraid of me," was the answer. "No," said the master, "it is because you have a murderous instinct." This dialogue recalls that of Soshi (Chuangtse), the Taoist. One day Soshi was walking on the bank of a river with a friend. "How delightfully the fishes are enjoying themselves in the water!" exclaimed Soshi. His friend spake to him thus: "You are not a fish; how do you know that the fishes are enjoying themselves?" "You are not myself," returned Soshi; "how do you know that I do not know that the fishes are enjoying themselves?"

Zen was often opposed to the precepts of orthodox Buddhism even as Taoism was opposed to Confucianism. To the transcendental insight of the Zen, words were but an incumbrance to thought; the whole sway of **Buddhist scriptures** only commentaries on personal speculation. The followers of Zen aimed at direct communion with the inner nature of things, regarding their outward accessories only as impediments to a clear perception of Truth. It was this love of the Abstract that led the Zen to prefer black and white sketches to the elaborately coloured paintings of the classic Buddhist School. Some of the Zen even became **iconoclastic** as a result of their endeavour to recognise the Buddha in themselves rather than through images and symbolism. We find Tankawosho breaking up a wooden statue of Buddha on a wintry day to make

▶舎利
【仏】仏陀の遺骨。

て、舎利を取ろうと思ったのだ」と和尚はおだやかに答えた。「仏像から舎利が取れるわけがない」と怒って反論すると、丹霞和尚はこう応じた。「もし舎利がとれなかったら、これはあきらかに仏陀ではないということだから、冒涜でもなんでもないではないか」 そう言うと、和尚は振り返って火にあたりはじめたという。

　禅が東洋思想に大きく貢献したのは、ありふれた日常の事が、精神的な事と同じくらい重要だと認めたことである。禅の考えによると、物事の関連性を大きくとらえれば、大小の区別はなく、一原子のなかにも宇宙と同じくらいの可能性がある。完全を求める人は自らの生活のなかに内面の光が反映されていることを発見しなくてはならない。この観点から考えると、禅林の仕組みというものはとても意義深いものである。祖師をのぞくすべての僧には、禅林の運営のための仕事が課せられ、妙なことに、新参者には軽い仕事が、修行を積み尊敬される僧には面倒な汚れ仕事が課せられるのである。このような勤めが禅修業の一部をなしており、どんな些細なことであっても完璧に果たされねばならない。このようにして、庭の草をむしりながら、蕪の皮をむきながら、お茶をいれながら、いくつもの重要な議論がつぎからつぎに起きた。茶道のいっさいの理想は、人生の些細な出来事の中に偉大なものを認識するという、この禅の考えからきているのである。道教は審美的理想の基礎を築き、禅はそれを実際的なものとしたのである。

a fire. "What sacrilege!" said the horror-stricken bystander. "I wish to get the Shali out of the ashes," calmly rejoined the Zen. "But you certainly will not get Shali from this image!" was the angry retort, to which Tanka replied, "If I do not, this is certainly not a Buddha and I am committing no sacrilege." Then he turned to warm himself over the kindling fire.

A special contribution of Zen to Eastern thought was its recognition of the mundane as of equal importance with the spiritual. It held that in the great relation of things there was no distinction of small and great, an atom possessing equal possibilities with the universe. The seeker for perfection must discover in his own life the reflection of the inner light. The organisation of the Zen monastery was very significant of this point of view. To every member, except the abbot, was assigned some special work in the care-taking of the monastery, and curiously enough, to the novices were committed the lighter duties, while to the most respected and advanced monks were given the more irksome and menial tasks. Such services formed a part of the Zen discipline and every least action must be done absolutely perfectly. Thus many a weighty discussion ensued while weeding the garden, paring a turnip, or serving tea. The whole ideal of Teaism is a result of this Zen conception of greatness in the smallest incidents of life. Taoism furnished the basis for æsthetic ideals, Zennism made them practical.

# 第 4 章　茶　室

## Chapter 4　The Tea-Room

石と煉瓦の建造物という伝統のなかで育った西洋の建築家にとって、木材や竹を用いる日本の建築方法は、建築とは見なしがたいのかもしれない。ある西洋建築の優れた研究者が、日本の大寺院の完成度の高さに注目してその価値を認めたのも、ほんの最近のことだ。日本のいにしえの建築物に関してさえその程度なので、外国人が茶室の**幽玄な美**を味わえるとはあまり期待できない。構造や装飾の理念が西洋のものとはまるで異なっているのである。

　茶室（「数寄屋」）は単なる茅葺きの小屋に過ぎない。「すきや」をあらわすもともとの漢字は「**好みの家（好き屋）**」という意味を持っていた。後世になり、茶人たちが茶室に対するそれぞれの考えに基づいて、さまざまな漢字を当てた。「すきや」という言葉はそれによって「**空き家（空虚な家）**」になったり、「**数奇屋（非対称の家）**」となったりした。詩情をその屋根の下にとどめる儚い物、という視点からは、それは「好き家」となる。いっときの美意識を満たすため以外には装飾がない、という意味では「空き家」となる。完成した姿について想像の余地を残すため、故意に何かを不完全にしておくという、未完を求める心のあらわれということにおいては「数奇

To European architects brought up on the traditions of stone and brick construction, our Japanese method of building with wood and bamboo seems scarcely worthy to be ranked as architecture. It is but quite recently that a competent student of Western architecture has recognised and paid tribute to the remarkable perfection of our great temples. Such being the case as regards our classic architecture, we could hardly expect the outsider to appreciate the **subtle beauty** of the tearoom, its principles of construction and decoration being entirely different from those of the West.

The tea-room (the Sukiya) does not pretend to be other than a mere cottage—a straw hut, as we call it. The original ideographs for Sukiya mean the **Abode of Fancy**. Latterly the various tea-masters substituted various Chinese characters according to their conception of the tea-room, and the term Sukiya may signify the **Abode of Vacancy** or the **Abode of the Unsymmetrical**. It is an Abode of Fancy inasmuch as it is an ephemeral structure built to house a poetic impulse. It is an Abode of Vacancy inasmuch as it is devoid of ornamentation except for what may be placed in it to satisfy some æsthetic need of the moment. It is an Abode of the Unsymmetrical inasmuch as it is consecrated to the worship of the Imperfect, purposely leaving some

屋」である。茶道の理念は16世紀以来、日本の一般的な建築にも影響を及ぼし、今日の日本家屋の内装の様式は、外国人にしてみるとほとんど何もないと思えるほど、非常に単純で簡素なものとなったのである。

▶千利休
▶千利休
1522–1591年、安土桃山時代の茶人。紹鷗に学び、日本の茶道を大成させたが、後年、秀吉の怒りに触れ自害する。

　最初に独立した茶室を建てたのは、のちに千利休として知られる茶人のなかの茶人、千宗易である。利休は16世紀に太閤秀吉の庇護のもとで茶の湯の作法を確立し、完成にまで高めた人物である。茶室の間取りは15世紀の有名な茶人紹鷗がすでに考案していた。初期の茶室はただ茶会をひらくために客間の一部を屏風で仕切ったものだった。仕切られた部屋は「囲い」と呼ばれ、いまでも別棟ではなく家屋のなかに設けられた茶室を「囲い」と呼んでいる。数寄屋は「グレース（美の三女神）よりは多く、ミューズ（芸術の九女神）よりは少ない」という言い回しでもわかるように、一度に5人ほどしか入れない茶室自体と、茶道具を出す前に洗って用意する控え室「水屋」、茶室に呼ばれるまで客人たちが待つ玄関「待合」、そして待合と茶室をつなぐ庭の小道「露地」から成っている。茶室は見た目には地味なものだ。日本の家屋で一番小さいものよりさらに小さく、使われている素材は清貧の趣をあらわすようなものである。しかしすべてこれは深遠な芸術的思慮のなせるものだということを忘れてはならない。どんなに壮

thing unfinished for the play of the imagination to complete. The ideals of Teaism have since the sixteenth century influenced our architecture to such a degree that the ordinary Japanese interior of the present day, on account of the extreme simplicity and chasteness of its scheme of decoration, appears to foreigners almost barren.

The first independent tea-room was the creation of Senno-Soyeki, commonly known by his later name of Rikiu, the greatest of all tea-masters, who, in the sixteenth century, under the patronage of Taiko-Hideyoshi, instituted and brought to a high state of perfection the formalities of the Tea-ceremony. The proportions of the tearoom had been previously determined by Jowo—a famous tea-master of the fifteenth century. The early tea-room consisted merely of a portion of the ordinary drawing-room partitioned off by screens for the purpose of the **tea-gathering**. The portion partitioned off was called the Kakoi (enclosure), a name still applied to those tea-rooms which are built into a house and are not independent constructions. The Sukiya consists of the tea-room proper, designed to accommodate not more than five persons, a number suggestive of the saying "more than the Graces and less than the Muses," an anteroom (midsuya) where the tea utensils are washed and arranged before being brought in, a portico (machiai) in which the guests wait until they receive the summons to enter the tearoom, and a garden path (the roji) which connects the machiai

麗な宮殿や寺院と比べても、それを凌ぐほど入念に細部にわたって仕上げられているのである。よい茶室というものは通常の住宅よりも建築費のかさむもので、**職人技**もさることながら、建築に使う材料はよく吟味され、確かな目で選び抜かれている。実際、茶人たちに雇われる大工は、職人のなかでも名誉のある高い地位を得ており、その仕事は漆家具の職人に勝るとも劣らない繊細さでおこなわれている。

　茶室はいずれの西洋建築とも異なっており、さらに日本の伝統的な建築と比べても著しく対照的である。日本の古くからの壮麗な建造物は、**宗教的なものであれ世俗的なもの**であれ、その大きさという点だけでも軽視することはできない。何世紀もの間、大火を免れてきた建物をみて、いまなおわれわれはその装飾の壮麗さ、豪華さに圧倒される。直径60〜90cm、高さ10m前後にもなる巨大な木の柱は、複雑に張り巡らされた木組みによって長大な梁を支え、その梁が傾斜のある瓦屋根の重みをしっかりと受けとめている。その素材と建築様式は、火災には弱いものの地震にはよく耐え、日本の気候に適したものである。法隆寺の金堂や薬師寺の塔は、まさに

with the tea-room. The tea-room is unimpressive in appearance. It is smaller than the smallest of Japanese houses, while the materials used in its construction are intended to give the suggestion of **refined poverty**. Yet we must remember that all this is the result of profound artistic forethought, and that the details have been worked out with care perhaps even greater than that expended on the building of the richest palaces and temples. A good tea-room is more costly than an ordinary mansion, for the selection of its materials, as well as its **workmanship**, requires immense care and precision. Indeed the carpenters employed by the tea-masters form a distinct and highly honoured class among artisans, their work being no less delicate than that of the makers of lacquer cabinets.

The tea-room is not only different from any production of Western architecture, but also contrasts strongly with the classical architecture of Japan itself. Our ancient noble edifices, whether **secular or ecclesiastical**, were not to be despised even as regards their mere size. The few that have been spared in the disastrous conflagrations of centuries are still capable of aweing us by the grandeur and richness of their decoration. Huge pillars of wood from two to three feet in diameter and from thirty to forty feet high, supported, by a complicated network of brackets, the enormous beams which groaned under the weight of the tile-covered slanting roofs. The material and mode of construction, though weak against fire, proved itself

木材建築の耐久性を証明する顕著な例であろう。これらは12世紀近くもの間、完全な姿をとどめて建っている。古い寺院や宮殿の内装はおどろくほど華美な装飾が施されている。10世紀に建てられた宇治の鳳凰堂（平等院）は、精巧な作りの天蓋と金箔を張った天井を持ち、鏡や螺鈿を象眼して多彩な色遣いがなされ、かつて壁面を飾った絵画や彫刻も残っている。時代を下って、日光東照宮や京都の二条城においては、構造の美はもはやあふれんばかりの装飾の犠牲となってしまった感もあるが、その色彩と凝った細部の造作はアラブやムーア式にみられる圧倒的な荘厳さに匹敵するほどだ。

▶天蓋
　仏像などを覆う装飾のこと。

▶螺鈿
　真珠色に光る貝殻を文様状にはめ込んだもの。

▶象眼
　鏡や貝殻をはめ込むこと。

▶ムーア
　元来はマグリブの先住民を指すが、15世紀頃からイスラム教徒一般を指すようになった。

　茶室の持つ簡潔さや純粋さは、禅林にならったことからきている。禅刹が他の仏教宗派と異なるのは、それがたんに僧侶たちの**住居**に過ぎないというところにある。本堂は礼拝や参拝の場ではなく、修行僧が問答のために集ったり、瞑想したりするための学舎である。そこにはなんの装飾もなく、仏壇の後ろの小さくへこんだ部分に宗祖である達磨大師の像か、初期の禅宗の指導者である迦葉と阿難陀を従えた釈迦の像が安置されているだけである。仏壇には、聖人たちの禅に対する功績を敬って香華が供えられている。達磨大師の像を前に、禅僧たちが茶を1個

▶禅刹
　禅宗の寺院。

▶香華
　香と花。

strong against earthquakes, and was well suited to the climatic conditions of the country. In the Golden Hall of Horiuji and the Pagoda of Yakushiji, we have noteworthy examples of the durability of our wooden architecture. These buildings have practically stood intact for nearly twelve centuries. The interior of the old temples and palaces was profusely decorated. In the Hoodo temple at Uji, dating from the tenth century, we can still see the elaborate canopy and gilded baldachinos, many-coloured and inlaid with mirrors and mother-of-pearl, as well as remains of the paintings and sculpture which formerly covered the walls. Later, at Nikko and in the Nijo castle in Kyoto, we see structural beauty sacrificed to a wealth of ornamentation which in colour and exquisite detail equals the utmost gorgeousness of Arabian or Moorish effort.

The simplicity and purism of the tea-room resulted from emulation of the Zen monastery. A Zen monastery differs from those of other Buddhist sects inasmuch as it is meant only to be a **dwelling place** for the monks. Its chapel is not a place of worship or pilgrimage, but a college room where the students congregate for discussion and the practice of meditation. The room is bare except for a central alcove in which, behind the altar, is a statue of Bodhi Dharma, the founder of the sect, or of Sakyamuni attended by Kashiapa and Ananda, the two earliest Zen patriarchs. On the altar, flowers and incense are offered up in memory of the

の碗から順に喫していくという儀式が茶の湯の起源になっている、ということは前に述べた。付け加えれば、禅寺の仏壇は、床の間の原型となった。床の間は、客人に鑑賞してもらうための絵画や花を飾る、和室において格別な位置を占める部分である。

偉大な茶人たちはおしなべてみな禅を修め、禅の精神を実生活に取り入れようと試みた。従って茶室は、他の茶道具と同様に、**禅の教義**を色濃く反映している。

正当な茶室の広さは4畳半（3m四方）で、これは維摩経の教典にある一節から定められた。この教典には、ヴィマラキールティが文殊師利菩薩と8万4000人の**仏弟子**をこの狭さの部屋でもてなした、という興味深い話がある。真の悟りを開いた者にとって、一切は皆空であるという教えの寓話だ。待合と茶室をつなぐ露地は、瞑想の第1段階——自己を目覚めさせる道——を象徴しているといえる。露地は外界とのつながりを断ち、新鮮な感受性を生み出すことで、茶室そのものにある美の趣向を深く味わう助けとなっている。この庭の小道に足を踏み入れれば、常緑の木々の薄明かりのなか、ばらばらのようで実は規則正しく並ぶ飛び石、その上に落ちかかる乾いた松葉を踏みしだき、苔むした御影石の灯

great contributions which these sages made to Zen. We have already said that it was the ritual instituted by the Zen monks of successively drinking tea out of a bowl before the image of Bodhi Dharma, which laid the foundations of the tea-ceremony. We might add here that the altar of the Zen chapel was the prototype of the Tokonoma,—the place of honour in a Japanese room where paintings and flowers are placed for the edification of the guests.

All our great tea-masters were students of Zen and attempted to introduce the spirit of Zennism into the actualities of life. Thus the room, like the other equipments of the tea-ceremony, reflects many of the **Zen doctrines**.

The size of the orthodox tea-room, which is four mats and a half, or ten feet square, is determined by a passage in the Sutra of Vikramadytia. In that interesting work, Vikramadytia welcomes the Saint Manjushiri and eighty-four thousand **disciples of Buddha** in a room of this size,—an allegory based on the theory of the non-existence of space to the truly enlightened. Again the roji, the garden path which leads from the machiai to the tea-room, signified the first stage of meditation,—the passage into self-illumination. The roji was intended to break connection with the outside world, and to produce a fresh sensation conducive to the full enjoyment of æstheticism in the tea-room itself. One who has trodden this garden path cannot fail to remember how his spirit, as he walked in the

籠の傍らを通るうちに、精神がふだんの思考を超えて高揚するのを覚えずにはいられない。都会のなかに居ながらにして、文明の塵と喧噪から遠く離れた森のなかにいるかのような心地になるだろう。このような静けさ、清らかさという効果を生み出す茶人の巧妙な企みには、舌を巻くしかない。露地をすぎるうちに得られる感覚は、茶人によってさまざまである。利休などの茶人はまったくの**孤愁**を目指し、露地を造る秘訣はつぎの古歌にあるとした。

▶藤原定家
　1162–1241年、鎌倉初期の公家、歌人。

見渡せば
花ももみぢも
なかりけり
浦の苫屋の
秋の夕暮れ

▶小堀遠州
　1579–1647年、近江小室藩藩主にして、茶人。作庭家としても名高い。

そのほか小堀遠州のような人は、別の効果を求めた。遠州は露地の理想が次のような句にみられるという。

夕月夜
海すこしある
木の間かな

twilight of evergreens over the regular irregularities of the stepping stones, beneath which lay dried pine needles, and passed beside the moss-covered granite lanterns, became uplifted above ordinary thoughts. One may be in the midst of a city, and yet feel as if he were in the forest far away from the dust and din of civilisation. Great was the ingenuity displayed by the tea-masters in producing these effects of serenity and purity. The nature of the sensations to be aroused in passing through the roji differed with different tea-masters. Some, like Rikiu, aimed at utter **loneliness**, and claimed the secret of making a roji was contained in the ancient ditty:

> *I looked beyond;*
> *Flowers are not,*
> *Nor tinted leaves.*
> *On the sea beach*
> *A solitary cottage stands*
> *In the waning light*
> *Of an autumn eve.*

Others, like Kobori-Enshiu, sought for a different effect. Enshiu said the idea of the garden path was to be found in the following verses:

> *A cluster of summer trees,*
> *A bit of the sea,*
> *A pale evening moon.*

遠州の意図するところを汲むのは難しいことではない。彼が創り出したかったのは、新たに目覚めようとする精神だろう。それはまだ過去のぼんやりとした夢のまにまに彷徨（さまよ）っているが、柔らかい心の光につつまれて無我の境地に浸りながら、彼方に広がる自由に憧れを感じている心なのだ。

このようにして、客人は心して聖域へと静かに向かう。もし武士であれば軒下の棚に刀を預けなければならない。茶室はこのうえない平和の場所だからだ。それから、高さが90センチもないような小さい入り口（躙口（にじりぐち））から、体を折るようにして茶室へにじり込む。身分に関わらず、いかなる客もこのように入室しなくてはならない。謙譲の精神を悟らせるためである。入室は、待合にいる間に客人同士で決めた順におこない、一人ずつ音を立てずに入って座り、床の間の絵や活花をまず鑑賞する。すべての客が座り、茶釜に湯がたぎる音以外に破るもののない静寂が訪れるとはじめて、主人が部屋に入る。釜が善い音を奏でる。釜の底に置かれた鉄片が独特の音を奏でるように造られているのだ。その快い調べに雲間からくぐもって聞こえる滝の響き、岩に打ち寄せる遠い潮騒、竹林を洗う驟雨、彼方の丘で風にざわめく松籟（しょうらい）、そういうものを客人たちは聞くのである。

日中でも部屋はほの暗い。斜めに造られた屋

▶ **驟雨**
急に降り出す雨、夕立。

▶ **松籟**
松に吹く風や、その音。

It is not difficult to gather his meaning. He wished to create the attitude of a newly-awakened soul still lingering amid shadowy dreams of the past, yet bathing in the sweet unconsciousness of a mellow spiritual light, and yearning for the freedom that lay in the expanse beyond.

Thus prepared the guest will silently approach the sanctuary, and, if a samurai, will leave his sword on the rack beneath the eaves, the tea-room being preeminently the house of peace. Then he will bend low and creep into the room through a small door not more than three feet in height. This proceeding was incumbent on all guests, —high and low alike,—and was intended to inculcate **humility**. The order of precedence having been mutually agreed upon while resting in the machiai, the guests one by one will enter noiselessly and take their seats, first making obeisance to the picture or **flower arrangement** on the tokonoma. The host will not enter the room until all the guests have seated themselves and quiet reigns with nothing to break the silence save the note of the boiling water in the iron kettle. The kettle sings well, for pieces of iron are so arranged in the bottom as to produce a peculiar melody in which one may hear the echoes of a cataract muffled by clouds, of a distant sea breaking among the rocks, a rainstorm sweeping through a bamboo forest, or of the soughing of pines on some faraway hill.

Even in the daytime the light in the room is

根は庇が低いため、日光はわずかしか入らない。天井から床まで、すべては地味な色合いを帯びている。客も地味な色あいの着物を入念に選んでいる。まわりは歳月を経てまろやかになったものばかりで、それと対照的にまっさらな竹の柄杓とまっ白な麻の茶巾以外、新しさを感じさせる物は避けられている。茶室と茶道具がどれほど古く色あせてみえようとも、すべては完璧に清潔でなければならない。暗がりの隅のほうであってもそこに塵ひとつとて落ちていてはいけない。もしあるようなら、その主人は茶人ではないということになる。茶人にまず求められるもののひとつが、掃き清めて洗う作法を心得ていることである。**掃除にも業**がある。年代物の金属細工を、オランダの主婦がするように手荒く扱ってはいけない。花瓶から滴った水は、ぬぐう必要はない。それは露や涼感を暗示するものになるからだ。

　ここで思い浮かぶのは、茶人が愉しんだ清潔感とはどんなものかをよくあらわしている利休の話だ。利休は息子の少庵が露地を掃いて水を打つのを見ていた。少庵が仕事をすませると、利休は「まだ充分ではない」といって再び庭を掃かせた。ほどなく疲れた息子は利休に告げた。「父上、これ以上できることはありません。庭石は3度も洗いましたし、灯籠と木には十分に水を撒きました。苔は青々と輝いています。地面には小枝1本、落葉1枚残っておりません」「たわけもの」と茶人は諭した。「露地はこのように掃くも

▶千少庵
　1546-1614年、利休の養子にして娘婿。茶人。

subdued, for the low **eaves** of the slanting roof admit but few of the sun's rays. Everything is sober in tint from the ceiling to the floor; the guests themselves have carefully chosen garments of unobtrusive colours. The mellowness of age is over all, everything suggestive of recent acquirement being tabooed save only the one note of contrast furnished by the bamboo dipper and the linen napkin, both immaculately white and new. However faded the tea-room and the tea-equipage may seem, everything is absolutely clean. Not a particle of dust will be found in the darkest corner, for if any exists the host is not a tea-master. One of the first requisites of a tea-master is the knowledge of how to sweep, clean, and wash, for there is an **art in cleaning** and dusting. A piece of antique metal work must not be attacked with the unscrupulous zeal of the Dutch housewife. Dripping water from a flower vase need not be wiped away, for it may be suggestive of dew and coolness.

In this connection there is a story of Rikiu which well illustrates the ideas of cleanliness entertained by the tea-masters. Rikiu was watching his son Shoan as he swept and watered the garden path. "Not clean enough," said Rikiu, when Shoan had finished his task, and bade him try again. After a weary hour the son turned to Rikiu: "Father, there is nothing more to be done. The steps have been washed for the third time, the stone lanterns and the trees are well sprinkled with water, moss and lichens are shining with a fresh verdure; not a twig, not a leaf have I left on the ground." "Young fool,"

のではない」　こういうと利休は庭に下り立って木を揺すり、金や紅の葉を落とし、秋の錦を庭に散り敷いた。利休は清潔感だけでなく、自然のなかの美をも求めていたのだ。


　「好き家」という言い方には、**一個人の美に対する欲求**を満たすために造る建物という意味がある。茶室は茶人のために造られたもので、茶室のために茶人があるのではない。後世に残す意図はなく、従ってつかの間のものである。人は皆自分の家を持つべきだという考え方は、日本民族の古くからの慣習に基づいたもので、神道の習わしでは、家長が死ねば、その住居は取り壊されなくてはならなかった。この慣習には何かしらの衛生上の理由もあったのかもしれない。この他にも古くからのならわしとして、新婚の二人には新築の家が与えられるということもあった。このような慣習のために、古代の日本ではかなり頻繁に都が遷されることになった。**日の神**（天照大神〈あまてらすおおみかみ〉）を祀る社、伊勢神宮が20年毎に遷宮をおこなうのも、今日に残る古来の儀式の一例である。この慣習を守っていくのは、容易に解体して建て直すことのできる木造建築という仕組みがあってこそ可能だった。煉瓦や石を用いるような建物が永く残る建築方法では、移動は非実用的なものになっていただろう。実際、奈良時代以降に、より頑丈で強固な木造建築が中国から伝えられてからは、移動もあまりおこなわ

chided the tea-master, "that is not the way a garden path should be swept." Saying this, Rikiu stepped into the garden, shook a tree and scattered over the garden gold and crimson leaves, scraps of the brocade of autumn! What Rikiu demanded was not cleanliness alone, but the beautiful and the natural also.

The name, Abode of Fancy, implies a structure created to meet some **individual artistic requirement**. The tea-room is made for the tea-master not the tea-master for the tea-room. It is not intended for posterity and is therefore ephemeral. The idea that everyone should have a house of his own is based on an ancient custom of the Japanese race, Shinto superstition ordaining that every dwelling should be evacuated on the death of its chief occupant. Perhaps there may have been some unrealised sanitary reason for this practice. Another early custom was that a newly built house should be provided for each couple that married. It is on account of such customs that we find the Imperial capitals so frequently removed from one site to another in ancient days. The rebuilding, every twenty years, of Ise Temple, the supreme shrine of the **Sun-Goddess**, is an example of one of these ancient rites which still obtain at the present day. The observance of these customs was only possible with some such form of construction as that furnished by our system of wooden architecture, easily pulled down, easily built up. A more lasting style, employing brick and stone, would have rendered migrations impracticable, as indeed they became when

れなくなった。


　15世紀に禅の個人主義が台頭すると、古くからの建築に対する考え方はより深い意味をもって茶室の概念と結びついた。禅は、**仏教の無常観**や、物質に対して精神が優位でなければならないという教えから、家屋というものは単に身を置くだけの仮の宿に過ぎないとみなした。身体そのものも荒れ野の一軒家でしかなく、手近な草を寄り合わせ、結んだ脆弱な小屋は、いったん解かれれば、またもとの荒れ野に還っていくものとされた。茅葺きの屋根や弱々しい細い柱、軽い竹の支え、ありきたりの材料を使った無造作な造り、そうしたものに茶室における儚さ<ruby>儚<rt>はかな</rt></ruby>さの表現をみることができるのだ。永遠というものはこうした簡素な四囲<ruby>囲<rt>し い</rt></ruby>に体現されていて、洗練さというほのかな光でその簡素さを美化する精神の内にこそみいだされるのである。


　茶室は個人的好みに適するように建てられるものだ、という考えは、芸術の活力が生まれる原則にかなっている。芸術が十分に鑑賞されるためには、その時代の生活にあてはまらなければならない。後世のことを考えないということではなく、現在をより楽しむようにしなくてはいけない。過去の創造を無視するのではなく、それを自分たちの意識のなかに取り込んで吸収しなくてはいけない。伝統と形式に**隷従**<ruby>隷従<rt>れいじゅう</rt></ruby>すれば、建築において個性を表現しようというときに足かせ

the more stable and massive wooden construction of China was adopted by us after the Nara period.

With the predominance of Zen individualism in the fifteenth century, however, the old idea became imbued with a deeper significance as conceived in connection with the tea-room. Zennism, with the **Buddhist theory of evanescence** and its demands for the mastery of spirit over matter, recognised the house only as a temporary refuge for the body. The body itself was but as a hut in the wilderness, a flimsy shelter made by tying together the grasses that grew around,—when these ceased to be bound together they again became resolved into the original waste. In the tea-room fugitiveness is suggested in the thatched roof, frailty in the slender pillars, lightness in the bamboo support, apparent carelessness in the use of commonplace materials. The eternal is to be found only in the spirit which, embodied in these simple surroundings, beautifies them with the subtle light of its refinement.

That the tea-room should be built to suit some individual taste is an enforcement of the principle of vitality in art. Art, to be fully appreciated, must be true to contemporaneous life. It is not that we should ignore the claims of posterity, but that we should seek to enjoy the present more. It is not that we should disregard the creations of the past, but that we should try to assimilate them into our consciousness. **Slavish conformity** to traditions and formulas fetters the expression of individuality in architecture. We can

となってしまう。今日の日本にみられるような、洋風建築を無分別に模倣したものは、嘆かわしいというしかない。先進的な西洋諸国で、建築がこれほどまでに独自性を持たず、旧来のスタイルを保ち続けているのは不思議なことだ。おそらく今日、芸術が民主化しようとする時代にいながら、新しい王朝を打ち立ててくれる君主のような師を待ち望んでいるのではないだろうか。古人を愛しみながらも、その真似のいよいよ少なからんことを！ ギリシャ人が偉大だといわれるのは、決して昔の模倣をしなかったためだ。

「空き家」という言葉は、すべてを内包するという道教の理念のほか、装飾のモチーフは常に変わるべきもの、という考えを含んでいる。茶室は何らかの美的な雰囲気を満たすために、一時的に置かれるもの以外、**虚空の空間**である。ときおり、特別な芸術品が持ち込まれることはあるが、その場合は他のものもこの第1の主題の美を引き立てるべく選ばれ、並べられる。複数の異なる音楽を一度に聴くことができないように、美を真に理解するためには、中心となるモチーフに集中しなくてはいけない。従って、茶室の装飾は、室内をしばしば美術館のように飾りたてる西洋のものとは対照的だ。簡素な装飾と、飾り付けを変えることに慣れている日本人からみると、絵画や彫刻、骨董品を恒常的にずらりと陳列した西洋の室内は、金持ちが持ち物を並べる低俗な趣味という印象を受けてしまう。1枚の名作でもたえずそれを眺めて楽しむにはかなりの

but weep over those senseless imitations of European buildings which one beholds in modern Japan. We marvel why, among the most progressive Western nations, architecture should be so devoid of originality, so replete with repetitions of obsolete styles. Perhaps we are now passing through an age of democratisation in art, while awaiting the rise of some princely master who shall establish a new dynasty. Would that we loved the ancients more and copied them less! It has been said that the Greeks were great because they never drew from the antique.

The term, Abode of Vacancy, besides conveying the Taoist theory of the all-containing, involves the conception of a continued need of change in decorative motives. The tea-room is **absolutely empty**, except for what may be placed there temporarily to satisfy some æsthetic mood. Some special art object is brought in for the occasion, and everything else is selected and arranged to enhance the beauty of the principal theme. One cannot listen to different pieces of music at the same time, a real comprehension of the beautiful being possible only through concentration upon some central motive. Thus it will be seen that the system of decoration in our tea-rooms is opposed to that which obtains in the West, where the interior of a house is often converted into a museum. To a Japanese, accustomed to simplicity of ornamentation and frequent change of decorative method, a Western interior permanently filled with a vast array of pictures, statuary, and

鑑賞力を必要とするし、ヨーロッパやアメリカの家庭によくあるような、色と形の洪水のなかで毎日を過ごせるというのは、芸術的感性の限度が底なしというしかないだろう。

「数寄屋（非対称の）」は、日本の装飾法におけるまた別の一面を示している。日本美術には左右対称性が欠けている、ということは西洋の批評家にしばしば指摘されてきた。これもまた、道教の思想が禅をとおしてあらわれた結果である。儒教とそのなかに深く根ざした二元論、また北方仏教の**三尊崇拝**では、対称の表現を排しているわけではない。実際のところ、古代中国の青銅器や、唐王朝や奈良時代の宗教美術品を研究すれば、対称性が追及されていた跡をみることができる。日本の古典的な室内装飾は、ものの配列に明らかな規則性があった。しかし、道教や禅の完全というものについての考え方は違っていた。その哲学は、完全そのものより、完全を追及する過程により重きを置くほどダイナミックなものであった。**不完全を完成させた者**のみが、真の美を見出すことができる。人生や芸術の力は、それが成長する可能性を秘めている点にこそあるというのだ。茶室では自己との関係において全体の効果を完成させることが、客の想像に任されている。禅が広く知られるようになると、極東の美術は、完全だけではなく反復をもあらわ

▶**三尊崇拝**
【仏】中央の中尊の左右に脇侍をおき崇拝すること。

bric-a-brac gives the impression of mere vulgar display of riches. It calls for a mighty wealth of appreciation to enjoy the constant sight of even a masterpiece, and limitless indeed must be the capacity for artistic feeling in those who can exist day after day in the midst of such confusion of colour and form as is to be often seen in the homes of Europe and America.

The "Abode of the Unsymmetrical" suggests another phase of our decorative scheme. The absence of symmetry in Japanese art objects has been often commented on by Western critics. This, also, is a result of a working out through Zennism of Taoist ideals. Confucianism, with its deep-seated idea of dualism, and Northern Buddhism with its **worship of a trinity**, were in no way opposed to the expression of symmetry. As a matter of fact, if we study the ancient bronzes of China or the religious arts of the Tang dynasty and the Nara period, we shall recognise a constant striving after symmetry. The decoration of our classical interiors was decidedly regular in its arrangement. The Taoist and Zen conception of perfection, however, was different. The dynamic nature of their philosophy laid more stress upon the process through which perfection was sought than upon perfection itself. True beauty could be discovered only by one who mentally **completed the incomplete**. The virility of life and art lay in its possibilities for growth. In the tea-room it is left for each guest in imagination to complete the total effect in relation to himself. Since Zennism has

すものとして、対称性を故意に避けるようになった。画一的なデザインは、新鮮な想像力を生みだすには致命的というわけだ。したがって、人物画よりも花鳥風月を描くことが好まれるようになった。人物は観賞者自身の人間性のなかにもあらわれるという点で画一性があるからだ。われわれはしばしば目立ちたがりすぎ、虚栄心があるにもかかわらず、自己認識は得てして単調なものになりがちなのである。

　茶室ではくり返しがあくまでも避けられる。部屋を飾るさまざまな品物は、色や意匠が重ならないように選ばれなくてはならない。もし活花があれば、花の絵は掛けてはならない。もし丸い釜を使うのであれば、水差しは角のあるものがよい。黒い釉薬の茶碗は黒漆の棗と同時に用いてはならない。花瓶や香炉を床の間に置くときには、それが空間を二分してしまうのを避けるため、ちょうど真ん中に置かないよう気をつけなくてはいけない。部屋が単調にならないように、床の間の柱には、他の柱とは違う種類の木材が使われる。

　ここでもまた、日本の室内装飾は西洋のそれとは異なっている。西洋では、品物が暖炉の上で左右対称に置かれる。西洋の住宅では、日本人にとっては意味のない反復と思われるものをよく目にする。話しかけようとする相手がいて、その等身大の肖像画が彼の背後からこちらを見つめ

▶釉薬
うわぐすりのこと。

▶棗
茶の入れ物。

become the prevailing mode of thought, the art of the extreme Orient has purposely avoided the symmetrical as expressing not only completion, but repetition. Uniformity of design was considered as fatal to the freshness of imagination. Thus, landscapes, birds, and flowers became the favourite subjects for depiction rather than the human figure, the latter being present in the person of the beholder himself. We are often too much in evidence as it is, and in spite of our vanity even self-regard is apt to become monotonous.

In the tea-room the fear of **repetition** is a constant presence. The various objects for the decoration of a room should be so selected that no colour or design shall be repeated. If you have a living flower, a painting of flowers is not allowable. If you are using a round kettle, the water pitcher should be angular. A cup with a black glaze should not be associated with a tea-caddy of black lacquer. In placing a vase or an incense burner on the tokonoma, care should be taken not to put it in the exact centre, lest it divide the space into equal halves. The pillar of the tokonoma should be of a different kind of wood from the other pillars, in order to break any suggestion of monotony in the room.

Here again the Japanese method of interior decoration differs from that of the Occident, where we see objects arrayed symmetrically on mantelpieces and elsewhere. In Western houses we are often confronted with what appears to us useless reiteration. We find it trying to talk to a man while his full-length portrait stares at us

ているのだ。絵の人物か、いま話している人物か、どちらが本物なのだろう。一方はにせものに違いない、という妙な確信を持ってしまう。祝いの席について、食堂の壁面を飾る贅沢な描写を眺めて、ひそかに食欲が失せてしまうことがある。なぜ、狩りの獲物を描き、魚や果物を丹念に彫刻してあるのだろう。なぜ、家伝の皿を並べるのだろう、かつてここで食事をしながらいまは亡き人々を思い出させるかのように。

茶室の簡素さや、俗悪なものを遠ざけた佇まいは、浮き世から離れた聖域である。茶室でのみ、なにものにも邪魔されることなく美を愛でることに没頭できる。16世紀には、日本の統一と再建に骨折った為政者や、勇猛な武士たちに、茶室は休息を与えた。17世紀に徳川家によって**厳格な儀式主義**が固められてからは、茶室は美の精神を自由に交感できる唯一の場となった。偉大な芸術の前には、大名も武士も平民も差別はない。今日、工業化によって、世界中で真の風雅を味わうことがますます難しいものになっている。いまこそ、われわれは茶室を必要としているのではないだろうか。

from behind his back We wonder which is real, he of the picture or he who talks, and feel a curious conviction that one of them must be fraud. Many a time have we sat at a festive board contemplating, with a secret shock to our digestion, the representation of abundance on the dining-room walls. Why these pictured victims of chase and sport, the elaborate carvings of fishes and fruit? Why the display of family plates, reminding us of those who have dined and are dead?

The simplicity of the tea-room and its freedom from vulgarity make it truly a sanctuary from the vexations of the outer world. There and there alone can one consecrate himself to undisturbed adoration of the beautiful. In the sixteenth century the tea-room afforded a welcome respite from labour to the fierce warriors and statesmen engaged in the unification and reconstruction of Japan. In the seventeenth century, after the **strict formalism** of the Tokugawa rule had been developed, it offered the only opportunity possible for the free communion of artistic spirits. Before a great work of art there was no distinction between daimyo, samurai, and commoner. Nowadays industrialism is making true refinement more and more difficult all the world over. Do we not need the tea-room more than ever?

# 第 5 章　芸術鑑賞

## Chapter 5　Art Appreciation

「琴馴らし」という道教徒の物語をご存じだろうか？

▶竜門の谷
　中国洛陽に位置し、竜門山と香山が対峙している。

　昔、竜門の谷にこれぞ真の森の王といわれた桐の樹があった。梢は星に語りかけるほどに伸び、根は地中深く突き進み、青銅色のとぐろを巻きながら、地の底に眠る銀竜にからみついていた。ある時、術に長けた妖術家がその樹から不思議な琴を作った。琴の精霊は頑迷固陋で、手なづけるには最高の弾き手の登場を待たねばならなかった。琴は長い間、皇帝の手元にあったが、その弦で調べを奏でようとする者たちの挑戦はことごとく退けられた。弾き手の懸命な努力にも、聞くに耐えない音色でしか応えず、ともに歌おうものなら、とげのある侮蔑の不協和音を響かせた。かくして琴は求める名手になかなか出会えなかったというわけだ。

▶頑迷固陋
　頑固で昔を知る老人の意。

　そんなとき、ついに伯牙という**琴の名手**があらわれた。暴れ馬をなだめようとするかのように、彼は優しく琴をなで、静かに弦に触れた。伯牙の手が自然や四季、そびえる山や川の流れを奏でると、なんと琴が樹であったころの記憶がよみがえったのだ！　再び心地よい春の息吹が桐の枝々の間で戯れる。峡谷をおどるように下っていく若々しい奔流が、芽吹いたばかりの花に笑いかける。時を移さず聞こえてきたのは夏の

Have you heard the Taoist tale of the Taming of the Harp?

Once in the hoary ages in the Ravine of Lungmen stood a Kiri tree, a veritable king of the forest. It reared its head to talk to the stars; its roots struck deep into the earth, mingling their bronzed coils with those of the silver dragon that slept beneath. And it came to pass that a mighty wizard made of this tree a wondrous harp, whose stubborn spirit should be tamed but by the greatest of musicians. For long the instrument was treasured by the Emperor of China, but all in vain were the efforts of those who in turn tried to draw melody from its strings. In response to their utmost strivings there came from the harp but harsh notes of disdain, ill-according with the songs they fain would sing. The harp refused to recognise a master.

At last came Peiwoh, the **prince of harpists**. With tender hand he caressed the harp as one might seek to soothe an unruly horse, and softly touched the chords. He sang of nature and the seasons, of high mountains and flowing waters, and all the memories of the tree awoke! Once more the sweet breath of spring played amidst its branches. The young cataracts, as they danced down the ravine, laughed to the budding flowers. Anon were heard the dreamy voices of summer

虫たちの大合唱、優しく降りそそぐ雨音、物悲しい郭公（かっこう）の鳴き声。さあ聞くがいい！　虎が咆哮（ほうこう）し、谷にこだましている。秋ともなれば寂しい夜に、剣（つるぎ）のごとく鋭い月が霜のおりた草地に輝く。冬の盛りは雪空に白鳥の群が旋回し、木々の枝には霰（あられ）が落ちて、歓喜の音を奏でる。

　伯牙がここで転調し、恋を歌いはじめると、物思いにふける恋人のように森が揺らぎだした。空では、とりすました乙女のように美しく輝く雲がたなびいたかと思えば、地上では失意のごとき長い影をひいて過ぎ去っていく。伯牙は再び調子を変えると、今度は戦いの調べを奏でた。剣戟（げき）の響きと蹄（ひづめ）の音。すると琴からは竜門に吹き荒れる嵐の音、竜が稲妻を御し、雪崩の轟音が山々に響き渡る。皇帝は感激し、伯牙に琴を鳴らす秘訣をたずねた。伯牙が答える。「陛下、他の人々はおのれのことばかり歌うのでうまくいかなかったのでしょう。私は琴に主題を委ねたのです。すると琴が伯牙なのか、伯牙が琴なのか自分でも判らなくなったのです」

　この物語は**芸術鑑賞**の極意をわかりやすく説明している。傑作とは見る者の琴線を奏でる交響楽なのだ。真の芸術は伯牙で、われわれは竜門の琴なのである。美の魔法に触れると、われわれの内なる弦が目を覚まし、呼びかけに応えて振動をはじめる。心が心に語りかける。無言のものに耳を傾け、見えないものを見つめる。名手は

with its myriad insects, the gentle pattering of rain, the wail of the cuckoo. Hark! a tiger roars,—the valley answers again. It is autumn; in the desert night, sharp like a sword gleams the moon upon the frosted grass. Now winter reigns, and through the snow-filled air swirl flocks of swans and rattling hailstones beat upon the boughs with fierce delight.

Then Peiwoh changed the key and sang of love. The forest swayed like an ardent swain deep lost in thought. On high, like a haughty maiden, swept a cloud bright and fair; but passing, trailed long shadows on the ground, black like despair. Again the mode was changed; Peiwoh sang of war, of clashing steel and trampling steeds. And in the harp arose the tempest of Lungmen, the dragon rode the lightning, the thundering avalanche crashed through the hills. In ecstacy the Celestial monarch asked Peiwoh wherein lay the secret of his victory. "Sire," he replied, "others have failed because they sang but of themselves. I left the harp to choose its theme, and knew not truly whether the harp had been Peiwoh or Peiwoh were the harp."

This story well illustrates the mystery of **art appreciation**. The masterpiece is a symphony played upon our finest feelings. True art is Peiwoh, and we the harp of Lungmen. At the magic touch of the beautiful the secret chords of our being are awakened, we vibrate and thrill in response to its call. Mind speaks to mind. We listen to the unspoken, we gaze upon the

われわれの知らない音色を呼び起こす。すると長く忘れていた記憶が新たな意味を携えてよみがえってくる。恐怖に押さえ込まれていた希望が、認める勇気のない憧憬が、新たな輝きの前にあらわれてくるのだ。われわれの心は画家が色を塗るキャンバスであり、彼らの使う絵具となるのが、われわれの感情なのだ。色彩の濃淡はすなわち、喜びの光であり、悲しみの影なのだ。傑作はわれわれ自身から生まれ、われわれは傑作から生まれるのだ。

　芸術を鑑賞するには心の交流が何より大切である。それは互いに譲り合う精神があってこそ成り立つといえる。芸術家が自らのメッセージを伝える術を心得ていなければならないのと同様に、鑑賞者もその投げかけを受け取る心構えを養っておく必要がある。お茶の宗匠である小堀遠州は、大名であったが、こんな言葉を残している。「名画を鑑賞するときは、名君に拝謁するのと同様にせよ」　傑作を理解するためには、身を低くし、息を殺し、一言半句も聞き漏らすまいとする気持ちが必要なのである。宋の有名な批評家が面白い告白をしている。彼いわく「若いころは、単に私が好む絵を描いた画家を褒めたが、鑑識眼が鍛えられると今度は、私が好きになるように画家が選んだものを、好きだと思える自分を褒めるようになった」　近ごろは、芸術家たちの心情を理解しようと心を砕く者がほとんどいないのは嘆かわしい限りだ。頑なに知ろうとしないで、このような簡単な礼儀も怠り、その

unseen. The master calls forth notes we know not of. Memories long forgotten all come back to us with a new significance. Hopes stifled by fear, yearnings that we dare not recognise, stand forth in new glory. Our mind is the canvas on which the artists lay their colour; their pigments are our emotions; their chiaroscuro the light of joy, the shadow of sadness. The masterpiece is of ourselves, as we are of the masterpiece.

The sympathetic communion of minds necessary for art appreciation must be based on mutual concession. The spectator must cultivate the proper attitude for receiving the message, as the artist must know to impart it. The tea-master, Kobori-Enshiu, himself a daimyo, has left to us these memorable words: "Approach a great painting as thou wouldst approach a great prince." In order to understand a masterpiece, you must lay yourself low before it and await with bated breath its least utterance. An eminent Sung critic once made a charming confession. Said he: "In my young days I praised the master whose pictures I liked, but as my judgment matured I praised myself for liking what the masters had chosen to have me like." It is to be deplored that so few of us really take pains to study the moods of the masters. In our stubborn ignorance we refuse to render them this simple courtesy, and thus often miss the rich repast of beauty spread before our very eyes. A master has always something to offer,

結果、目の前に広がっている贅沢な美の供応を味わい損なうことになるのだ。芸術家はいつでもご馳走の用意をしているのに、われわれにそれを味わう術がなく、空腹のままでいることになる。

　傑作を身近に感じることができれば、それが実在のものとなり、まるで友だちになったような心地になるものだ。芸術家は不滅である。それは彼らの愛も悲しみも、世代を超えてわれわれのなかに生きているからだ。われわれを引きつけてやまないのは、彼らの腕よりもむしろ魂であり、技術ではなく人間性なのだ。訴えかけるものが人間的であればあるほどわれわれの心に深く届く。作者との間にこうした**暗黙の了解**があるからこそ、われわれは詩や小説で主人公とともに悩み喜ぶことができるのだ。日本のシェイクスピアともいうべき近松門左衛門は、戯曲の構成上なくてはならない要素として、作者だけが知っている秘密に、観客を誘い込むことが重要だといっている。ある時、数人の弟子が近松に戯曲をみてもらったところ、気に入られたのは１作品だけだった。それは『間違いの喜劇』に似た筋立で、双子の兄弟が間違えられて苦労するという内容だった。近松は「この作品には、芝居に必要な心がある。客の視線だ。客というのは役者なんぞよりずっと物知りだ。どこで行き違いが起きるのかちゃんとわかっていて、罪もないのに運命に押し流されていく**舞台上**の人物に同情するものなんだよ」と言った。

▶**近松門左衛門**
　江戸中期の浄瑠璃、歌舞伎脚本の作者。義理人情を題材に人間の心を描いた。

▶**『間違いの喜劇』**
　1594年、シェイクスピア作の戯曲。

while we go hungry solely because of our own lack of appreciation.

To the sympathetic a masterpiece becomes a living reality towards which we feel drawn in bonds of comradeship. The masters are immortal, for their loves and fears live in us over and over again. It is rather the soul than the hand, the man than the technique, which appeals to us,—the more human the call the deeper is our response. It is because of this **secret understanding** between the master and ourselves that in poetry or romance we suffer and rejoice with the hero and heroine. Chikamatsu, our Japanese Shakespeare, has laid down as one of the first principles of dramatic composition the importance of taking the audience into the confidence of the author. Several of his pupils submitted plays for his approval, but only one of the pieces appealed to him. It was a play somewhat resembling the Comedy of Errors, in which twin brethren suffer through mistaken identity. "This," said Chikamatsu, "has the proper spirit of the drama, for it takes the audience into consideration. The public is permitted to know more than the actors. It knows where the mistake lies, and pities the poor figures **on the board** who innocently rush to their fate."

西洋でも東洋でも巨匠は、観客にそれとなく秘密を知らせる手段としての**暗示**の大切さを忘れたことはなかった。傑作をじっくり鑑賞すれば誰でも思いが無限に広がり、畏敬の念が湧いてくる。なんと親しみ深く心が通じ合っていることだろう。それにひきかえ、現代の作品はありふれていて、いかにも冷ややかだ。巨匠の作品には人の心の暖かみがあふれているが、現代作品には型通りの挨拶程度しか感じない。技術一辺倒の現代人はおのれを超えることなど滅多にない。竜門の琴を呼び覚ませなかった楽人のように、おのれのことしか奏でないのである。彼らの作品は科学に近づくばかりで、人間性からはほど遠くなっている。日本の古い諺に「うぬぼれ男に惚れてはならぬ」というのがある。いくら愛を注いでも、うぬぼれ男の心には他人の愛が入り込む余地などないということだ。芸術も同じで、うぬぼれは決して共感を生まない。芸術家にとっても鑑賞者にとっても致命的なものなのである。

　芸術において似かよった精神と精神がひとつになることほど尊いものはない。その瞬間、芸術を愛する者は自己を超越するのだ。そして存在すると同時に存在しない状態になる。そのとき彼は**無限**をちらっとかいま見るが、その喜びは声にならない。目には舌がないからだ。精神は物質の呪縛から解放され、もののリズムで動くようになる。芸術は宗教に近くなり、人を気高くする。傑作が神聖なものになる瞬間である。昔の日本人が偉大な芸術家の作品に抱いた尊敬の気持

The great masters both of the East and the West never forgot the value of **suggestion** as a means for taking the spectator into their confidence. Who can contemplate a masterpiece without being awed by the immense vista of thought presented to our consideration? How familiar and sympathetic are they all; how cold in contrast the modern commonplaces! In the former we feel the warm outpouring of a man's heart; in the latter only a formal salute. Engrossed in his technique, the modern rarely rises above himself. Like the musicians who vainly invoked the Lungmen harp, he sings only of himself. His works may be nearer science, but are further from humanity. We have an old saying in Japan that a woman cannot love a man who is truly vain, for there is no crevice in his heart for love to enter and fill up. In art vanity is equally fatal to sympathetic feeling, whether on the part of the artist or the public.

Nothing is more hallowing than the union of kindred spirits in art. At the moment of meeting, the art lover transcends himself. At once he is and is not. He catches a glimpse of **Infinity**, but words cannot voice his delight, for the eye has no tongue. Freed from the fetters of matter, his spirit moves in the rhythm of things. It is thus that art becomes akin to religion and ennobles mankind. It is this which makes a masterpiece something sacred. In the old days the veneration in which the Japanese held the work of the great artist

ちは大きなものだった。茶の宗匠は名品を守る
ため、絹布でそっと包み込み、さらに幾重にも箱
を重ね、あくまでも聖なるものを守るよう扱っ
た。そうした秘蔵品は免許皆伝のとき以外、人目
に触れることもまれだった。

▶免許皆伝
奥義を伝えるこ
と。

　茶道が盛んだった時代、太閤秀吉の武将たち
は戦勝の褒美として広大な領地より貴重な名品
を贈られることを喜んだという。わが国で長く
親しまれている芝居には、名品を紛失したり取
り返したりする話が数多くある。たとえばこん
な話がある。細川家の城には雪村が描いた有名
な達磨の絵があった。ところが警護にあたって
いた侍の不注意で、火災が起きてしまう。何とし
ても貴重な絵を救いたいと思った侍は、燃えさ
かる城に飛び込み目的の掛物を手にしたが、す
べての逃げ道は炎で塞がれていた。絵を助ける
ことしか頭にない侍は、おのれの刀でわが身を
切り開き、裂いた袖に掛軸をくるんでその傷に
押し込んだ。ようやく火事がおさまり、まだけぶ
る焼跡には侍の死体が焼け残っていた。ところ
が、体内からは秘蔵の掛軸が無傷で見つかった
のだ。悲惨な話だが、信頼を背負った侍の**忠節心**
はもとより、日本人がいかに芸術品を重んじて
いるかがよくわかる。

　しかし、忘れてはならないのは、芸術の価値は
われわれに訴えかけてくるものがどれほどある

was intense. The tea-masters guarded their treasures with religious secrecy, and it was often necessary to open a whole series of boxes, one within another, before reaching the shrine itself—the silken wrapping within whose soft folds lay the holy of holies. Rarely was the object exposed to view, and then only to the initiated.

At the time when Teaism was in the ascendency the Taiko's generals would be better satisfied with the present of a rare work of art than a large grant of territory as a reward of victory. Many of our favourite dramas are based on the loss and recovery of a noted masterpiece. For instance, in one play the palace of Lord Hosokawa, in which was preserved the celebrated painting of Dharuma by Sesson, suddenly takes fire through the negligence of the samurai in charge. Resolved at all hazards to rescue the precious painting, he rushes into the burning building and seizes the kakemono, only to find all means of exit cut off by the flames. Thinking only of the picture, he slashes open his body with his sword, wraps his torn sleeve about the Sesson, and plunges it into the gaping wound. The fire is at last extinguished. Among the smoking embers is found a half-consumed corpse, within which reposes the treasure un-injured by the fire. Horrible as such tales are, they illustrate the great value that we set upon a masterpiece, as well as the **devotion** of a trusted samurai.

We must remember, however, that art is of value only to the extent that it speaks to us. It might be a

かで決まるということだ。われわれが時と場所を超えて心に感じることができれば、芸術は**普遍的な言語**だといえよう。だが、われわれの生まれもった性質、伝統や因習、そして遺伝的な本能——こうしたものが芸術を楽しむ能力を狭めているのである。ある意味で個性こそが芸術鑑賞に限界を与えている。つまり、われわれは美を見極めようとするとき、過去の作品に類似点を求めてしまうのである。確かに研鑽を積むことで芸術鑑賞の能力が高まり、これまで気づかなかった美の表現を楽しめるようになるかもしれない。だが結局のところ、われわれは宇宙のなかに自分の姿をみているだけなのだ。感じ方というのは個人の持つ特性によって決まってしまうものなのである。茶の宗匠にしても自分の眼鏡にかなった物だけを収集しているにすぎない。

小堀遠州がこんな逸話を残している。遠州の収集品の趣味の良さに弟子たちが感服し、褒めそやした。「どれをとってみてもじつに見事といわざるを得ません。利休に勝るほどの見る目がおありになる。何しろ利休の集める品を誉めるのは1000人に１人でしたから」 遠州は情けない思いで答えた。「それは私がいかに**凡俗**かという証です。偉大なる利休師はご自身がお感じになるものだけを大切になさった。それにひきかえ私は知らぬうちに周囲の大多数に迎合していた。まさしく、利休師こそ千人に一人の大宗匠でありました」

**universal language** if we ourselves were universal in our sympathies. Our finite nature, the power of tradition and conventionality, as well as our hereditary instincts, restrict the scope of our capacity for artistic enjoyment. Our very individuality establishes in one sense a limit to our understanding; and our æsthetic personality seeks its own affinities in the creations of the past. It is true that with cultivation our sense of art appreciation broadens, and we become able to enjoy many hitherto unrecognised expressions of beauty. But, after all, we see only our own image in the universe,—our particular idiosyncrasies dictate the mode of our perceptions. The tea masters collected only objects which fell strictly within the measure of their individual appreciation.

One is reminded in this connection of a story concerning Kobori-Enshiu. Enshiu was complimented by his disciples on the admirable taste he had displayed in the choice of his collection. Said they, "Each piece is such that no one could help admiring. It shows that you had better taste than had Rikiu, for his collection could only be appreciated by one beholder in a thousand." Sorrowfully Enshiu replied: "This only proves how **commonplace** I am. The great Rikiu dared to love only those objects which personally appealed to him, whereas I unconsciously cater to the taste of the majority. Verily, Rikiu was one in a thousand among tea-masters."

昨今の芸術熱はうわべだけのもので、本物の感情に根ざしていないのが残念でならない。この民主主義という時代では、自分がどう思うかでなく、世間が良いと考えるものに人が殺到している。人々は洗練されたものより値段の張るものを、美しいものより流行のものを求める。大衆が芸術に触れようとするとき、工業主義の生産物である**絵入りの雑誌**を眺めるほうが、知ったかぶりをしてイタリア初期の作品や足利時代の名品を鑑賞するよりとっつきやすいのだろう。作品の質よりも芸術家の名前ばかりが重要視されている。何世紀も前に、中国のある批評家が「人々は耳で絵画の価値を決めている」と嘆いたという。**古典主義擬き**がいま盛んにもてはやされているのは、まともな鑑賞能力が欠如しているからである。

　芸術と考古学を混同してしまうという間違いもよく起こる。古いものを敬う気持ちは人間の優れた特性のひとつであり、さらに高めていきたいものである。古の巨匠は、後世の文化が発展する途を開いたのだから尊敬されて当たり前だ。何世紀にもおよんで批評を受けながらもわれわれの時代に受け継がれ、なおも栄光に包まれているという事実だけでも尊敬に値する。しかし、ただ時代を重ねているというだけで価値があるとみなすとしたら、まったく愚かしいことである。にもかかわらず、われわれは時代の重みに思わず負けて、美的感覚をないがしろにしている。われわれは芸術家が天寿をまっとうすれば、花

It is much to be regretted that so much of the apparent enthusiasm for art at the present day has no foundation in real feeling. In this democratic age of ours men clamour for what is popularly considered the best, regardless of their feelings. They want the costly, not the refined; the fashionable, not the beautiful. To the masses, contemplation of **illustrated periodicals**, the worthy product of their own industrialism, would give more digestible food for artistic enjoyment than the early Italians or the Ashikaga masters, whom they pretend to admire. The name of the artist is more important to them than the quality of the work. As a Chinese critic complained many centuries ago, "People criticise a picture by their ear." It is this lack of genuine appreciation that is responsible for the **pseudo-classic** horrors that today greet us wherever we turn.

Another common mistake is that of confusing art with archaeology. The veneration born of antiquity is one of the best traits in the human character, and fain would we have it cultivated to a greater extent. The old masters are rightly to be honoured for opening the path to future enlightenment. The mere fact that they have passed unscathed through centuries of criticism and come down to us still covered with glory commands our respect. But we should be foolish indeed if we valued their achievement simply on the score of age. Yet we allow our historical sympathy to override our æsthetic discrimination. We offer flowers of approbation when the artist is safely laid in his grave. The nineteenth

を手向ける。19世紀になり**進化論**が盛んになると、種における個人を見なくなってしまったのだ。収集家は一時代、あるいは一流派を説明するための見本集めに夢中になり、数多くの凡作よりただひとつの傑作のほうが多くのことを教えてくれることを忘れてしまった。分類することに必死になり過ぎて、芸術を少しも楽しんでいない。系統立てて展示することで美的要素が損なわれているのは、多くの美術館が抱えている弊害である。

　いかなる人生を送ろうと、現代芸術の主張を無視することはできない。今日の芸術はまさしくわれわれのものであり、われわれの姿を映している。それを非難することはおのれを非難することに他ならない。現代に芸術など存在しないというが、それは誰の責任だろう？　昔の人々には熱狂的な賛辞を贈りながら、われわれ自身の可能性には知らぬふりを決め込むなど恥ずべきことである。芸術家たちはもがきながらも、冷ややかな侮蔑の暗闇をさまよい続けている。自分本位なこの時代、われわれは芸術家の創造意欲をかき立てているだろうか？　過去は現代文明の貧しさに呆れ、未来は現代芸術の不毛さをあざ笑うだろう。われわれは生活のなかの美を破壊することで芸術をも破壊している。偉大な妖術家があらわれて、現代社会の幹から類い稀なる琴を作り出し、天才の手で音色を響かせてくれたならば……。

century, pregnant with the **theory of evolution**, has moreover created in us the habit of losing sight of the individual in the species. A collector is anxious to acquire specimens to illustrate a period or a school, and forgets that a single masterpiece can teach us more than any number of the mediocre products of a given period or school. We classify too much and enjoy too little. The sacrifice of the æsthetic to the so-called scientific method of exhibition has been the bane of many museums.

The claims of contemporary art cannot be ignored in any vital scheme of life. The art of today is that which really belongs to us: it is our own reflection. In condemning it we but condemn ourselves. We say that the present age possesses no art:—who is responsible for this? It is indeed a shame that despite all our rhapsodies about the ancients we pay so little attention to our own possibilities. Struggling artists, weary souls lingering in the shadow of cold disdain! In our self-centred century, what inspiration do we offer them? The past may well look with pity at the poverty of our civilisation; the future will laugh at the barrenness of our art. We are destroying art in destroying the beautiful in life. Would that some great wizard might from the stem of society shape a mighty harp whose strings would resound to the touch of genius.

# 第6章 活 花
Chapter 6　Flowers

春の曙の薄明のなか、木々の梢で神秘的なさ
えずりを交わす小鳥の声を聞くとき、あなたは
小鳥たちが仲間に向かって花のことを語ってい
るのだと感じたことはないだろうか。人間も、愛
の詩を詠んだのと同じころから花を鑑賞してい
たにちがいない。その無邪気さゆえに美しく、沈
黙ゆえに芳しい一輪の花ほど、乙女の魂が解き
放たれる姿を想像させるものはあるだろうか?

　原始時代の人間は乙女にはじめて花輪を捧げ
たとき、その**獣性**から脱却した。人はそのように
して、自然界のありのままの状態を超えて人間
らしくなったのである。無用と思っていたものに
多少の使い道があると気づいたとき、人は芸術
の領域に入るのである。

　楽しいときも、悲しいときも花はわれわれの
変わらぬ友である。われわれは花とともに食べ、
飲み、歌い、踊り、戯れる。結婚式も命名の式も
花とともにある。花なくしては死におよぶことさ
えできないだろう。百合を崇め、蓮とともに瞑想
し、薔薇や菊とともに戦列に居並ぶ。**花言葉**で話
そうとさえする。花なくしてどうして生きていか
れようか。花のない世界を想像するだけでも恐
ろしい。病める人の枕辺に、花はどれほどの慰め
をもたらしてくれることか。疲れた心の闇に、花
は**至福の光**をもたらしてくれる。そのたおやか

In the trembling grey of a spring dawn, when the birds were whispering in mysterious cadence among the trees, have you not felt that they were talking to their mates about the flowers? Surely with mankind the appreciation of flowers must have been coeval with the poetry of love. Where better than in a flower, sweet in its unconsciousness, fragrant because of its silence, can we image the unfolding of a virgin soul? The primeval man in offering the first garland to his maiden thereby transcended **the brute**. He became human in thus rising above the crude necessities of nature. He entered the realm of art when he perceived the subtle use of the useless.

In joy or sadness, flowers are our constant friends. We eat, drink, sing, dance, and flirt with them. We wed and christen with flowers. We dare not die without them. We have worshipped with the lily, we have meditated with the lotus, we have charged in battle array with the rose and the chrysanthemum. We have even attempted to speak in the **language of flowers**. How could we live without them? It frightens one to conceive of a world bereft of their presence. What solace do they not bring to the bedside of the sick. What **a light of bliss** to the darkness of weary spirits?

さは、愛らしい子どもをみていると失われた希望がよみがえってくるように、この世への失いかけた信頼を取り戻してくれる。われわれが地面深くに横たわるときも、悲しみをもって墓に置かれるのは花である。

悲しいことに、常に花とともにありながら、われわれがその獣性から抜け出ていないという事実を隠すことはできない。羊の皮を剥いでみれば、その内にある狼が牙をむく。人は10歳では獣、20歳で狂人、30歳で落伍者、40歳で山師、50歳で罪人になるといわれている。おそらくは獣性を脱することができないゆえに罪人となるのだろう。人間にとって飢えよりも生々しいものはなく、自身の欲望ほど大事なものはない。神社仏閣は目の前でつぎつぎと崩壊していくが、ひとつの祭壇だけは永遠に残され、そのうえでわれわれは至高の偶像神のために香を焚くのである。その神とは、われわれ自身である。この神は偉大であり、金銭こそがその予言者なのだ！　われわれはその神に生贄を捧げるために自然を荒らすのである。物質を征服したといって自慢し、物質こそがわれわれを奴隷としていることは忘れている。文化と進歩の名のもとに、われわれはなんという暴虐の限りを尽くしていることか！

教えておくれ、優しい花よ、星の雫よ、お前たちは庭に立ち、露と日光を称えて歌う蜜蜂に向かってうなずいているが、お前たちを待ち受けている恐ろしい運命に気づいているのだろうか？　いまのうちに夢をみて、穏やかな夏のそ

Their serene tenderness restores to us our waning confidence in the universe even as the intent gaze of a beautiful child recalls our lost hopes. When we are laid low in the dust it is they who linger in sorrow over our graves.

Sad as it is, we cannot conceal the fact that in spite of our companionship with flowers we have not risen very far above the brute. Scratch the sheepskin and the wolf within us will soon show his teeth. It has been said that man at ten is an animal, at twenty a lunatic, at thirty a failure, at forty a fraud, and at fifty a criminal. Perhaps he becomes a criminal because he has never ceased to be an animal. Nothing is real to us but hunger, nothing sacred except our own desires. Shrine after shrine has crumbled before our eyes; but one altar forever is preserved, that whereon we **burn incense** to the supreme **idol**,—ourselves. Our god is great, and money is his **Prophet**! We devastate nature in order to make sacrifice to him. We boast that we have conquered Matter and forget that it is Matter that has enslaved us. What atrocities do we not perpetrate in the name of culture and refinement!

Tell me, gentle flowers, teardrops of the stars, standing in the garden, nodding your heads to the bees as they sing of the dews and the sunbeams, are you aware of the fearful doom that awaits you? Dream on, sway and frolic while you may in the gentle breezes of

よ風のなかで揺れて浮かれているがよい。明日になれば**無慈悲な手**がお前たちの喉を絞めるだろう。もぎ取られ、手足をばらばらにされて、静かな住処（すみか）から連れ去られてしまうだろう。そんなことをするあさましい人間は、通りすがりの美人であるかもしれない。なんと美しい花でしょう、と感嘆する間にも、その手はお前たちの血で濡れているのである。これが優しさというものだろうか。無情な人間の髪にとめられるか、お前の顔を見ようともしない人のボタンの穴に挿されるのが、お前の宿命かもしれない。喉が渇いているのにそれを潤すこともできない濁った水を張った窮屈な器に押し込まれるのが、お前の宿命なのかもしれないのだ。

　花よ、もしお前たちがミカドの国に住んでいるのなら、ときに鋏（はさみ）と小型の鋸（のこぎり）を持った恐ろしい人間と出会うことがあるかもしれない。

　その人間は**活花の師匠**と自称している。自分は花の医者だと主張するが、お前たちは本能的に彼を嫌うに違いない。医者というのは常に患者の苦しみを引き延ばそうとするものだと知っているからだ。彼はお前たちを切り取り、折り曲げ、自分がこれがよいと思う無理な形になるまで細工するが、お前たちはそれを耐え忍ばなければならない。彼は整体師のようにお前たちの筋をねじ曲げ、脱臼させる。出血を止めようとして真っ赤に燃える炭火を押しつけ、循環を助けるといっては針金を突き刺す。塩や、酢や、明礬（みょうばん）、ときには硫酸までも与えようとする。気絶

summer. Tomorrow a **ruthless hand** will close around your throats. You will be wrenched, torn asunder limb by limb, and borne away from your quiet homes. The wretch, she may be passing fair. She may say how lovely you are while her fingers are still moist with your blood. Tell me, will this be kindness? It may be your fate to be imprisoned in the hair of one whom you know to be heartless or to be thrust into the buttonhole of one who would not dare to look you in the face were you a man. It may even be your lot to be confined in some narrow vessel with only stagnant water to quench the maddening thirst that warns of ebbing life.

Flowers, if you were in the land of the Mikado, you might some time meet a dread personage armed with scissors and a tiny saw.

He would call himself a **Master of Flowers**. He would claim the rights of a doctor and you would instinctively hate him, for you know a doctor always seeks to prolong the troubles of his victims. He would cut, bend, and twist you into those impossible positions which he thinks it proper that you should assume. He would contort your muscles and dislocate your bones like any osteopath. He would burn you with red-hot coals to stop your bleeding, and thrust wires into you to assist your circulation. He would diet you with salt, vinegar, alum, and sometimes, vitriol. Boiling water would be poured on your feet when you seemed ready

しそうになれば、煮え湯を足元に注ぐ。こうして、自らの手当てによって2週間かそれ以上も長くお前たちを生かしておくことができたといって自慢するわけだ。それならば、最初に囚われの身となったときにひと思いに死んだほうがましだったとは思わないか? このような罰を受けて当然だというなら、前世でどのような罪を犯したためだというのだろうか?

西欧社会における気まぐれな花の浪費ぶりは、東洋の活花の師匠よりもさらにひどい。ヨーロッパやアメリカで舞踏会場や宴席を飾るために毎日のように切られ、翌日になれば捨てられてしまう花の量は莫大なものである。それらの花を繋ぎ合わせれば、ゆうに一大陸を花の輪で飾ることができよう。このように花の命をまったく無頓着に扱うことに比べれば、活花の師匠の罪などは取るに足らないものかもしれない。彼は少なくとも、自然に敬意を表して、それを無闇に浪費することはせず、切るべき花を選ぶのにも慎重で、花が枯れてしまえば、礼をもってその残骸を扱うからである。西欧では、花を飾ることは富を誇示する虚飾の一部であり、一時の気まぐれに過ぎないように思われる。お祭り騒ぎが終われば、これらの花はどこへいってしまうのだろうか? 色褪せた花が芥の山に無惨にも投げ捨てられているのをみるほど哀れなものはない。

花はなぜそれほど美しく儚いものとして生まれたのだろうか。虫は刺すことができるし、おとなしそうな動物でも、追いつめられれば戦う。帽

to faint. It would be his boast that he could keep life within you for two or more weeks longer than would have been possible without his treatment. Would you not have preferred to have been killed at once when you were first captured? What were the crimes you must have committed during your past incarnation to warrant such punishment as this?

The wanton waste of flowers among Western communities is even more appalling than the way they are treated by Eastern Flower-Masters. The number of flowers cut daily to adorn the ballrooms and banquet tables of Europe and America, to be thrown away on the morrow, must be something enormous; if strung together they might garland a continent. Beside this utter carelessness of life, the guilt of the Flower-Master becomes insignificant. He, at least, respects the economy of nature, selects his victims with careful foresight, and after death does honour to their remains. In the West the display of flowers seems to be a part of the pageantry of wealth,—the fancy of a moment. Whither do they all go, these flowers, when the revelry is over? Nothing is more pitiful than to see a faded flower remorselessly flung upon a dung heap.

Why were the flowers born so beautiful and yet so hapless? Insects can sting, and even the meekest of beasts will fight when brought to bay. The bird whose

子の飾り用に羽根を狙われる鳥は、飛んで逃げることができるし、毛皮目当てに狩られる動物は、追っ手が近づけば隠れることができる。悲しいかな！　翼を持つ花は蝶だけである。その他の花はいずれも、略奪者に対して無防備に立ち尽くすほかはない。もし花が**断末魔**の叫びをあげたとしても、その声はわれわれの無情な耳には達しない。黙ってわれわれを愛し、仕えてくれるものたちに対して、われわれは残忍な態度を取り続けてきた。それゆえに、もっとも親しい友からも見捨てられる日が来るのかもしれない。野の花が年々少なくなっていることにお気づきではないだろうか？　花のなかの賢者が、われわれがもっと人間らしくなる日まではこの世を去るほうが賢明だと説いているかのようである。もしかしたら、花はすでに天に移り住んでしまったのかもしれないのだ。

　花を栽培する人には、もっと高い評価を与えてもいいだろう。鉢植えを楽しむ人は、鋏を持つ者よりもはるかに人情味にあふれている。水や日光に気を配り、寄生虫を駆除し、霜を恐れ、蕾が出るのが遅いといっては心配し、葉につやが出てきたといっては喜ぶ人をみるのは楽しいものだ。東洋において、**花卉の栽培技術**は長い歴史を持つ。詩人たちとその好みの花への愛着ぶりは、しばしば物語や詩歌にも記されている。唐代から宋代の陶磁器の発展とともに、花を植えるための見事な花器が造られたことはよく知られている。それは単なる鉢ではなく、宝石で

▶花卉
　鑑賞のための草や花。

plumage is sought to deck some bonnet can fly from its pursuer, the furred animal whose coat you covet for your own may hide at your approach. Alas! The only flower known to have wings is the butterfly; all others stand helpless before the destroyer. If they shriek in their death **agony** their cry never reaches our hardened ears. We are ever brutal to those who love and serve us in silence, but the time may come when, for our cruelty, we shall be deserted by these best friends of ours. Have you not noticed that the wild flowers are becoming scarcer every year? It may be that their wise men have told them to depart till man becomes more human. Perhaps they have migrated to heaven.

Much may be said in favour of him who cultivates plants. The man of the pot is far more humane than he of the scissors. We watch with delight his concern about water and sunshine, his feuds with parasites, his horror of frosts, his anxiety when the buds come slowly, his rapture when the leaves attain their lustre. In the East the **art of floriculture** is a very ancient one, and the loves of a poet and his favourite plant have often been recorded in story and song. With the development of ceramics during the Tang and Sung dynasties we hear of wonderful receptacles made to hold plants, not pots, but jewelled palaces. A special attendant was detailed

飾られた宮殿のようなものであった。それぞれの花に仕える世話係がいて、その葉を兎の毛でできた柔らかな刷毛（はけ）で洗ったという。牡丹には美しく盛装した侍女が水をやり、寒梅には色白でやせた僧が水をやったという記録が残っている。日本において、もっとも有名な能の舞のひとつ「鉢の木」という演目が足利時代にできている。これは、寒い夜に燃やす薪がなくて凍えていた貧しい武士が、旅の**托鉢僧**をもてなすために、大事にしていた鉢植えを切るという物語に基づいている。この托鉢僧はじつは日本におけるハールーン・アッラシード──北条時頼その人であった。そしてこの犠牲は報われるのだ。この能は今日の東京でも上演され、そのたびに観客の涙を誘わずにはおかない。

か弱い花を保護するために、さまざまな配慮がなされた。唐の玄宗帝（げんそう）は、花園から鳥を追い払うために、木々の枝に小さな金の鈴を吊るした。春になると、妙なる音楽で花たちを喜ばせようと、宮廷の楽人たちを伴って花園を訪れたのもこの帝であった。日本におけるアーサー王ともいうべき源義経が書いたとされる奇妙な高札が、日本のある寺に現存する。それは見事な梅の木を守るために立てられた警告であり、戦乱の世独特の残酷なユーモアでわれわれの心に訴える。その梅花の美しさを誉め称えたあとに、こう書かれている。「ひと枝を伐（と）らば一指を剪（き）るべき（この枝を1本なりと切った者は指1本を切られるべし）」。今日でも、みだりに花を切ったり、芸

▶『鉢の木』
　世阿弥（能を大成した人物）の父、観阿弥（1333-84）の作という説が残っているが、定かではない。

▶ハールーン・アッラシード
　766-809年、アッバース朝の第5代帝王。アラビア語の説話集『アラビアン・ナイト』にも登場する。

▶高札
　禁令などを伝えた掲示板。

▶須磨寺
　現神戸市にある福祥寺の通称。

to wait upon each flower and to wash its leaves with soft brushes made of rabbit hair. It has been written that the peony should be bathed by a handsome maiden in full costume, that a winter-plum should be watered by a pale, slender monk. In Japan, one of the most popular of the No-dances, the Hachinoki, composed during the Ashikaga period, is based upon the story of an impoverished knight, who, on a freezing night, in lack of fuel for a fire, cuts his cherished plants in order to entertain a wandering **friar**. The friar is in reality no other than Hojo-Toki-yori, the Haroun-Al-Raschid of our tales, and the sacrifice is not without its reward. This opera never fails to draw tears from a Tokio audience even today.

Great precautions were taken for the preservation of delicate blossoms. Emperor Huensung, of the Tang dynasty, hung tiny golden bells on the branches in his garden to keep off the birds. He it was who went off in the springtime with his court musicians to gladden the flowers with soft music. A quaint tablet, which tradition ascribes to Yoshitsune, the hero of our Arthurian legends, is still extant in one of the Japanese monasteries. It is a notice put up for the protection of a certain wonderful plum-tree, and appeals to us with the grim humour of a warlike age. After referring to the beauty of the blossoms, the inscription says: "Whoever cuts a single branch of this tree shall forfeit a finger therefor." Would that such laws could be enforced

術品を損傷したりする者には、こんな法律を適用すべきなのだ！

だが、鉢植えの花についてさえ、人間の身勝手さを感じるときがある。なぜ花をそのふるさとから移して、見知らぬ環境で咲かせようとするのか。まるで小鳥を籠に閉じ込めて歌わせたり、番わせたりするのと同じことではないか。蘭の花が温室の人工的な熱気に息をつまらせながら、ふるさとの南国の空をひと目見たいとかなわぬ望みを抱いていることを誰が知ろう。

理想的な花の愛好家とは、花のもともとの住処を訪れる人のことである。破れた竹垣の前にすわって野菊と語らった陶淵明のように。または、黄昏の西湖のほとりに咲く梅の花のなかをさまよいつつ、その妙なる香りにわれを忘れた林和靖のように。周茂叔は、蓮の花と渾然一体の夢を見るために小舟のなかで眠ったといわれている。奈良の都のもっとも名高い后である光明皇后のみ心を動かしたのも、このような心であった。皇后はこう詠まれている。「折りつればたぶさにけがるたてながら三世の仏に花たてまつる（花よ、もしお前を摘めば、わが手はお前を汚してしまうだろう。あるがままに草原に立つお前を、わたしは過去、現在、未来の仏に捧げよう）」

だが、あまり感傷的になるのはやめよう。贅沢ばかりいうのではなく、もっと大きくとらえようではないか。老子は「**天地不仁**（天地は慈悲の心を持たない）」という。弘法大師いわく「生まれ、生まれ、生まれ、生まれて、命の流れはたゆ

▶陶淵明
365–427年、六朝時代の詩人（東晋）。

▶林和靖
967–1028年、宋代の詩人。

▶周茂叔
1017–1073年、宋時代の儒学者。

nowadays against those who wantonly destroy flowers and mutilate objects of art!

Yet even in the case of pot flowers we are inclined to suspect the selfishness of man. Why take the plants from their homes and ask them to bloom mid strange surroundings? Is it not like asking the birds to sing and mate cooped up in cages? Who knows but that the orchids feel stifled by the artificial heat in your conservatories and hopelessly long for a glimpse of their own Southern skies?

The ideal lover of flowers is he who visits them in their native haunts, like Taoyuen-ming, who sat before a broken bamboo fence in converse with the wild chrysanthemum, or Linwosing, losing himself amid mysterious fragrance as he wandered in the twilight among the plum-blossoms of the Western Lake. 'Tis said that Chowmushih slept in a boat so that his dreams might mingle with those of the lotus. It was this same spirit which moved the Empress Komio, one of our most renowned Nara sovereigns, as she sang: "If I pluck thee, my hand will defile thee, O Flower! Standing in the meadows as thou art, I offer thee to the Buddhas of the past, of the present, of the future."

However, let us not be too sentimental. Let us be less luxurious but more magnificent. Said Laotse: "**Heaven and earth are pitiless**." Said Kobodaishi: "Flow, flow, flow, flow, the current of life is ever onward. Die, die, die, die, death comes to all." Destruction faces

みなく進んで行く。死に、死に、死んで、死んで、死はすべてのものに訪れる」。まわりをみれば至るところに破壊がある。下にも上にも、後ろにも前にもそれは存在する。永遠なるものは変転のみ——であればなぜ命と同じく死をも迎えないのか？　どちらも互いの片割れではないか——梵天（ブラーマ）の昼と夜ではないか。古いものの崩壊があってはじめて創造が可能になる。われわれは容赦ない慈悲の女神である「死」に、さまざまな名を与えてこれを崇めてきた。それは**拝火教徒**が火中に見た「すべてを滅ぼすもの」の影であった。今日でも神道が身を伏せる剣の魂のように冷酷な純粋主義である。神秘の火はわれわれの弱さを焼き尽くし、聖なる剣は欲望の束縛を断ち切る。われわれの違灰から、天上の希望という不死鳥が生まれ出る。その解放から、より高次の人格が誕生するのである。

　花を切ることによって、世界理念を高尚なものにする新しい形を生み出すことができるなら、そうしても構わないのではないだろうか。われわれはただ、花とともに美への献上をしたいだけなのだ。われわれ自身が**清浄と簡素**に身を捧げることによって罪滅ぼしをする。このような理屈で、茶人は**活花**を造り上げたのである。

　わが国の茶や花の宗匠の作法についてよく知っている人なら、彼らが宗教的な崇敬の念をもって花を扱うことに気づいているだろう。みだりに花を摘むことはせず、心に思う花の美的な構成を考えながら、注意深くそれぞれの枝を選

us wherever we turn. Destruction below and above, destruction behind and before. Change is the only Eternal,—why not as welcome Death as Life? They are but counterparts one of the other,—the Night and Day of Brahma. Through the disintegration of the old, re-creation becomes possible. We have worshipped Death, the relentless goddess of mercy, under many different names. It was the shadow of the All-devouring that the **Gheburs** greeted in the fire. It is the icy purism of the sword-soul before which Shinto-Japan prostrates herself even today. The mystic fire consumes our weakness, the sacred sword cleaves the bondage of desire. From our ashes springs the phoenix of celestial hope, out of the freedom comes a higher realisation of manhood.

Why not destroy flowers if thereby we can evolve new forms ennobling the world idea? We only ask them to join in our sacrifice to the beautiful. We shall atone for the deed by consecrating ourselves to **Purity and Simplicity**. Thus reasoned the tea-masters when they established the **Cult of Flowers**.

Anyone acquainted with the ways of our tea and flower-masters must have noticed the religious veneration with which they regard flowers. They do not cull at random, but carefully select each branch or spray with an eye to the artistic composition they

ぶのであり、必要以上に花を切ることがあれば恥じ入るばかりなのだ。このために、葉が少しでもある場合は、葉と花をあわせて扱う。植物全体の美しさを表現することがその目的だからである。他の事柄と同様、この点をみても日本の花の扱いは、西欧の国々とは異なっている。西欧では、花梗（花をつける枝）だけが乱雑に花瓶に挿されているのをよくみかける。

　茶の宗匠は思い通りに花を活けると、日本間においては上座とされる床の間にそれを飾る。花の効果を妨げるようなものは一切その近くには置かない。とくに美的な効果があると思われる場合をのぞけば、花と絵を組み合わせて飾ることもないのだ。花は玉座に就いた皇子のようにその場所に置かれ、訪れた客や弟子たちは、主人に挨拶する前に、まず花に向かってうやうやしくお辞儀をするのである。できばえのよかった活花は、愛好家の理解を深めるために、絵に描かれ、本として数多く出版されているほどだ。そして、花が色褪せると、宗匠はそれをそっと川に流すか、または丁寧に地中に埋める。ときには花を偲んで碑が建てられることさえある。

　華道の誕生は、15世紀の茶道のそれと時を同じくしている。伝えられるところによれば、最初の活花は、生きとし生けるものすべてに心遣いをする仏教僧が、嵐で散らばった花を集めて、水を張った器に入れたものとされている。また足

have in mind. They would be ashamed should they chance to cut more than were absolutely necessary. It may be remarked in this connection that they always associate the leaves, if there be any, with the flower, for their object is to present the whole beauty of plant life. In this respect, as in many others, their method differs from that pursued in Western countries. Here we are apt to see only the flower stems, heads, as it were, without body, stuck promiscuously into a vase.

When a tea-master has arranged a flower to his satisfaction he will place it on the tokonoma, the **place of honour** in a Japanese room. Nothing else will be placed near it which might interfere with its effect, not even a painting, unless there be some special æsthetic reason for the combination. It rests there like an enthroned prince, and the guests or disciples on entering the room will salute it with a profound bow before making their addresses to the host. Drawings from master-pieces are made and published for the edification of amateurs. The amount of literature on the subject is quite voluminous. When the flower fades, the master tenderly consigns it to the river or carefully buries it in the ground. Monuments even are sometimes erected to their memory.

The birth of the Art of Flower Arrangement seems to be simultaneous with that of Teaism in the fifteenth century. Our legends ascribe the first flower arrangement to those early Buddhist saints who gathered the flowers strewn by the storm and, in their infinite

利義政の時代に活躍した画家であり、鑑定家でもあった相阿弥が、初期の華道における名人であったと伝わっている。茶人の珠光もその門弟の一人であった。また池坊の開祖である専能もその弟子である。池坊一派は、画家の一族として名高い狩野家に引けを取らない名門である。16世紀後半、利休によって茶の湯の儀式が完成をみたのにともない、華道もまためざましい発展を遂げた。利休とその流れをくむ人々、有名な織田有楽、古田織部、光悦、小堀遠州、片桐石州などは、競って新しい取合せを試みた。だが、茶人の花への崇敬は、茶の湯における美的な儀式の一部に過ぎず、それ自体で独立したものではなかったということも覚えておかなくてはならない。活花は、茶室における他の美術品と同じく、装飾全体のなかにおいては従属するものであった。石州は、庭に雪が積っているときには白梅を用いてはならないと定めた。「けばけばしい」花は容赦なく茶室から遠ざけられた。茶人による活花は、その線や周囲との調和が特に考慮して仕上げられているため、意図して置かれた場所から動かされてしまうと、とたんにその意味を失ってしまうのだ。

　花それ自体を崇めることは、17世紀中ごろ、「花の宗匠」があらわれたころに端を発する。それは茶室からは独立するようになり、器との調和のほかにはとくに制約はなくなった。その創

solicitude for all living things, placed them in vessels of water. It is said that Soami, the great painter and connoisseur of the court of Ashikaga-Yoshimasa, was one of the earliest adepts at it. Juko, the tea-master, was one of his pupils, as was also Senno, the founder of the house of Ikenobo, a family as illustrious in the annals of flowers as was that of the Kanos in painting. With the perfecting of the tea-ritual under Rikiu, in the latter part of the sixteenth century, flower arrangement also attains its full growth. Rikiu and his successors, the celebrated Oda-Wuraku, Furuta-Oribe, Koyetsu, Kobori-Enshiu, Katagiri-Sekishiu, vied with each other in forming new combinations. We must remember, however, that the flower worship of the tea-masters formed only a part of their æsthetic ritual, and was not a distinct religion by itself. A flower arrangement, like the other works of art in the tea-room, was subordinated to the total scheme of decoration. Thus Sekishiu ordained that white plum blossoms should not be made use of when snow lay in the garden. "Noisy" flowers were relentlessly banished from the tea-room. A flower arrangement by a teamaster loses its significance if removed from the place for which it was originally intended, for its lines and proportions have been specially worked out with a view to its surroundings.

The adoration of the flower for its own sake begins with the rise of "**Flower-Masters**," toward the middle of the seventeenth century. It now becomes independent of the tea-room and knows no law save that the

造には新しい概念や扱いが可能となり、そこから結果として多くの原則や流派が生まれるに至った。19世紀中ごろのある文筆家は、華道には百以上もの異なった流派があると述べている。大まかにいえば、これらは**「形式派」**と**「写実派」**の二大流派に分けられる。池坊の率いる形式派は、狩野派に相当する古典的な理想主義を目指していた。この派の初期の宗匠たちの作品の記録が残っているが、それらは山雪や常信の描く花卉を再現したかのようである。一方で写実派は、その名の示す通り、自然をその師と仰いでいた。美的な統一感を表現しうるときに限って、形の修正を施すのであった。そのために写実派の作品には、浮世絵や四条派の絵に巧まれたのと同じような意匠がみられる。

▶**山雪、常信**
狩野山雪と狩野常信。狩野派の絵師。

▶**四条派**
京都の四条に住んだ呉春を祖とする日本画の一派。

時間が許すならば、この時代のさまざまな花の宗匠によって定められた構成や細則について、さらに調べてみるのも興味深いことである。ここに徳川時代の装飾法を支配していた基本的な理論がみられる。そこには**指導する原理**（天）、**従属する原理**（地）、**和解する原理**（人間）への言及が認められる。これらの原理を体現していない活花はすべて貧弱で枯れたも同然のものとみなされた。また、花を活けるには、正式、半正式、略式の3つの側面に分けて扱うことが大事であるとも述べられている。第1は舞踏会における

vase imposes on it. New conceptions and methods of execution now become possible, and many were the principles and schools resulting therefrom. A writer in the middle of the last century said he could count over one hundred different schools of flower arrangement. Broadly speaking, these divide themselves into two main branches, the **Formalistic** and the **Naturalesque**. The Formalistic schools, led by the Ikenobos, aimed at a classic idealism corresponding to that of the Kano-academicians. We possess records of arrangements by the early masters of this school which almost reproduce the flower paintings of Sansetsu and Tsunenobu. The Naturalesque school, on the other hand, as its name implies, accepted nature as its model, only imposing such modifications of form as conduced to the expression of artistic unity. Thus we recognise in its works the same impulses which formed the Ukiyoe and Shijo schools of painting.

It would be interesting, had we time, to enter more fully than is now possible into the laws of composition and detail formulated by the various flower-masters of this period, showing, as they would, the fundamental theories which governed Tokugawa decoration. We find them referring to the **Leading Principle** (Heaven), the **Subordinate Principle** (Earth), the **Reconciling Principle** (Man), and any flower arrangement which did not embody these principles was considered barren and dead. They also dwelt much on the importance of treating a flower in its three different aspects, the

盛装、第2は午後のゆったりとした優雅な装い、第3は私室の小粋な普段着に相当する。


　われわれの個人的な好みからすれば、花の宗匠の活花より、むしろ茶人の活花のほうに共感を覚える。茶人による活花は、花を正しく扱うやり方であって、日常と深く交わっているという点で心にせまってくる。これを写実派や形式派と区別して、**自然派**と呼んでもよいだろう。茶人は自らの役目は花の選定で終わるものと考え、あとは花自身に自らを語らせる。晩冬の茶室に入れば、山桜の細枝にまだ蕾の椿が取合わせてあるのが見られるだろう。それは去りゆく冬を送り、来るべき春を迎える呼びかけなのである。また、苛立つほど暑い夏、昼時の茶に招かれてみれば、床の間のほの暗く涼しい空間に吊るされた花活けに、一輪の百合を見るだろう。まだ露に濡れたその百合は、人生の愚かさを微笑んでいるかのようである。

　花の独奏も目に楽しいものであるが、絵画や彫刻とともに協奏曲を奏でるとき、その取合せは人をうっとりさせる。石州はあるとき、水盤に水草を活けて湖沼の草木を模し、その上の壁に相阿弥の描くところの空飛ぶ鴨の絵を掲げた。茶人の紹巴は、海辺のわびしい美しさを詠んだ歌を漁夫の小屋の形をした青銅の香炉と取合

Formal, the Semi-Formal, and the Informal. The first might be said to represent flowers in the stately costume of the ballroom, the second in the easy elegance of afternoon dress, the third in the charming dishabille of the boudoir.

Our personal sympathies are with the flower-arrangements of the tea-master rather than with those of the flower-master. The former is art in its proper setting and appeals to us on account of its true intimacy with life. We should like to call this school the **Natural** in contradistinction to the Naturalesque and Formalistic schools. The teamaster deems his duty ended with the selection of the flowers, and leaves them to tell their own story. Entering a tea-room in late winter, you may see a slender spray of wild cherries in combination with a budding camellia; it is an echo of departing winter coupled with the prophecy of spring. Again, if you go into a noon-tea on some irritatingly hot summer day, you may discover in the darkened coolness of the tokonoma a single lily in a hanging vase; dripping with dew, it seems to smile at the foolishness of life.

A solo of flowers is interesting, but in a concerto with painting and sculpture the combination becomes entrancing. Sekishiu once placed some water plants in a flat receptacle to suggest the vegetation of lakes and marshes, and on the wall above he hung a painting by Soami of wild ducks flying in the air. Shoha, another tea-master, combined a poem on the Beauty of Solitude

せ、それに海浜の野花を添えた。客の一人は、その取合せ全体に過ぎゆく秋の息遣いを感じたと書き残している。

　花にまつわる逸話には限りがないが、もうひとつだけ紹介しよう。16世紀の日本においては、朝顔はまだ珍しい花だった。利休は庭全体を朝顔で埋め尽くして、**丹精こめて世話**をしていた。その朝顔の評判が太閤秀吉の耳にも入り、太閤はそれを見たいと所望した。そこで利休は太閤を自宅の朝の茶に招待した。当日、やってきた太閤は庭を歩いたが、朝顔は跡形もなくなっていた。地面はならされ、美しい小石や砂が撒かれていた。太閤は不興の面持ちで茶室に入ったが、そこにあるものをみて、すっかり上機嫌になった。床の間に宋代の珍しい青銅の器が置かれ、そこにただ一輪の庭の女王ともいうべき朝顔の花が咲いていたのである。

▶**花御供**
　神仏に花を供えること。

　このような例を知れば、「花御供（はなごくう）」の意味するところがよくわかる。おそらく花もその意味を知っていることだろう。花は人間のように臆病ではない。**死することを誇り**としている花もある。風に散りゆく日本の桜がまさにそれである。吉野や嵐山の匂いたつような花吹雪のなかに立てば、そのことを感じるだろう。桜は束の間、宝石を散りばめた雲のように空に浮かび、清流の水面に舞う。そして、さざめく水の流れに乗って

by the Sea with a bronze incense burner in the form of a fisherman's hut and some wild flowers of the beach. One of the guests has recorded that he felt in the whole composition the breath of waning autumn.

Flower stories are endless. We shall re-count but one more. In the sixteenth century the morning-glory was as yet a rare plant with us. Rikiu had an entire garden planted with it, which he cultivated with **assiduous care**. The fame of his convolvuli reached the ear of the Taiko, and he expressed a desire to see them, in consequence of which Rikiu invited him to a morning tea at his house. On the appointed day the Taiko walked through the garden, but nowhere could he see any vestige of the convolvulus. The ground had been leveled and strewn with fine pebbles and sand. With sullen anger the despot entered the tearoom, but a sight waited him there which completely restored his humour. On the tokonoma, in a rare bronze of Sung workmanship, lay a single morning-glory—the queen of the whole garden!

In such instances we see the full significance of the **Flower Sacrifice**. Perhaps the flowers appreciated the full significance of it. They are not cowards, like men. Some flowers **glory in death**—certainly the Japanese cherry blossoms do, as they freely surrender themselves to the winds. Anyone who has stood before the fragrant avalanche at Yoshino or Arashiyama must have realised this. For a moment they hover like bejewelled clouds and dance above the crystal streams; then, as they

流れていく。「さらば、春よ！　われわれは永遠
の旅に出る」と言っているようである。

sail away on the laughing waters, they seem to say: "Farewell, O Spring! We are on to Eternity."

# 第7章 茶 人
Chapter 7 Tea-Masters

宗教では、未来はわれらの背後にある。芸術では現在こそが永遠である。茶人は、芸術を真に理解できるのは芸術から日々影響を受ける者だけだと考えた。だからこそ日々の生活を、茶室で得られるような高度に洗練された規範で律しようとしたのだ。どのような状況でも**心の平穏**を保ち、会話が周囲の調和を乱すことがあってはならない。着物の形や色も姿勢も歩き方も、すべてその人の芸術的な表現となりうる。これらを軽々しく扱ってはいけない。おのれを美しくすることなくして、美へ到達することはできないからだ。そうしてこそ、茶人は芸術家であることを超え、芸術そのものに近づこうとする。それこそが**禅の美学**である。完璧なものは、見つけることさえできればいたるところにあるものだ。利休は好んで次の古歌を引用した。「花をのみ　待つらん人に　山里の　雪間の草の　春を見せばや」

▶**藤原家隆**
1158-1237年、鎌倉時代初期の歌人。

茶人の芸術への貢献は多岐にわたる。それまでの古典的な建築と内装に改革をもたらし、まったく新しい型を確立したのは茶人である。それは「茶室」の章で述べたとおりである。その影響は、16世紀以降に建てられたあらゆる宮殿や

In religion the Future is behind us. In art the Present is the eternal. The tea-master held that real appreciation of art is only possible to those who make of it a living influence. Thus they sought to regulate their daily life by the high standard of refinement which obtained in the tea-room. In all circumstances **serenity of mind** should be maintained, and conversation should be so conducted as never to mar the harmony of the surroundings. The cut and colour of the dress, the poise of the body, and the manner of walking could all be made expressions of artistic personality. These were matters not to be lightly ignored, for until one has made himself beautiful he has no right to approach beauty. Thus the tea-master strove to be something more than the artist,—art itself. It was the **Zen of æstheticism**. Perfection is everywhere if we only choose to recognise it. Rikiu loved to quote an old poem which says: "To those who long only for flowers, fain would I show the full-blown spring which abides in the toiling buds of snow-covered hills"

Manifold indeed have been the contributions of the tea-masters to art. They completely revolutionised the classical architecture and interior decorations, and established the new style which we have described in the chapter of the tea-room, a style to whose influence

寺院にみられる。たとえば小堀遠州はその**異能ぶり**を桂離宮や名古屋城、二条城、そして孤逢庵などの建築にいかんなく発揮している。また日本の有名な庭園はことごとく茶人の設計による。日本の陶器も、茶人の与えた着想がなければ、その高みに到達しえなかっただろう。茶の湯の席で用いられる道具づくりには、わが国の陶芸家たちの創意工夫が最大限に発揮されている。日本の陶芸の研究者で、いわゆる「遠州七窯」を知らぬ者はない。織物の多くには、その色調や柄を考案した茶人の名がつけられている。わが国の芸術で、茶人がその才能の一端を刻印していない分野をみつけることは不可能に近いといえるだろう。絵画や漆塗りの世界にも茶人が多大な貢献をなしていることはいうまでもないだろう。日本画の主要な流派のひとつは、漆塗りや陶芸の達人としても知られた茶人本阿弥光悦を祖としている。光悦の偉業と並べば、その孫光甫や、甥の子光琳や乾山のすばらしい作品もほとんど霞んでしまうほどだ。そもそも、いわゆる琳派の絵画そのものが茶道精神の表現といっていい。琳派にみられる太い線に、人は自然の生命力そのものを感じとれるはずだ。

▶**遠州七窯**
　小堀遠州が好んだ茶器の7ヵ所の産地。

▶**本阿弥光悦**
　1558–1637年、江戸初期に活躍した芸術家。

▶**琳派**
　江戸中期の画家、尾形光琳と同傾向の表現方法を用いる派。

　茶人が芸術の分野に与えた影響の大きさも、それが人の生きざまに与えた影響に比べれば小

even the palaces and monasteries built after the sixteenth century have all been subject. The **many-sided** Kobori-Enshiu has left notable examples of his genius in the Imperial villa of Katsura, the castles of Nagoya and Nijo, and the monastery of Kohoan. All the celebrated gardens of Japan were laid out by the tea-masters. Our pottery would probably never have attained its high quality of excellence if the tea-masters had not lent to it their inspiration, the manufacture of the utensils used in the tea-ceremony calling forth the utmost expenditure of ingenuity on the part of our ceramists. The Seven Kilns of Enshiu are well known to all students of Japanese pottery. Many of our textile fabrics bear the names of tea-masters who conceived their colour or design. It is impossible, indeed, to find any department of art in which the tea-masters have not left marks of their genius. In painting and lacquer it seems almost superfluous to mention the immense service they have rendered. One of the greatest schools of painting owes its origin to the tea-master Honnami-Koyetsu, famed also as a lacquer artist and potter. Beside his works, the splendid creation of his grandson, Koho, and of his grand-nephews, Korin and Ken-zan, almost fall into the shade. The whole Korin school, as it is generally designated, is an expression of Teaism. In the broad lines of this school we seem to find the vitality of nature herself.

Great as has been the influence of the tea-masters in the field of art, it is as nothing compared to that which

さいものだ。礼節を重んじる社会の風習はもちろん、日常のこまごました決めごとにも茶人たちの存在が感じられる。和食の繊細な料理もその供し方も、その多くは茶人たちの創案である。彼らは日本人に、地味な色の服だけを着るよう教えた。花に接するときの正しい精神も教えてくれた。素朴さを愛する自然な心を大切にせよと説き、謙譲の美徳を示した。こうした教えを通じて、茶の心は日本人の生活に浸透していったのである。

人生という愚かな苦渋の大海に漕ぎ出し、荒波にもまれる自らをどう律するか、その奥義を知らぬ者は、うわべの幸せをとりつくろうとしても虚しく、たえず惨めな状態にあるものだ。われわれは心の安定を求めてはつまずき、水平線に浮かぶ雲には嵐の前兆をみる。しかし永遠（とわ）へと逆巻く荒波にも喜びと美しさがあるものだ。その精神に身を委ね、あるいは列子（れっし）のように嵐に跳び乗るもいいではないか。

▶列子
　中国、春秋戦国時代の道家、思想家。

美しく生きた者のみが美しく死ぬことができる。偉大な茶人たちの死に際は、その生涯に負けぬほど、極度に洗練されていた。宇宙の偉大なリズムとの調和を常に求めてきたから、彼らにはいつでも未知なる世界へ入っていく覚悟があった。「**利休、最後の一服**」は、その悲劇的な壮絶さゆえに永遠に記憶されるであろう。

利休と豊臣秀吉は古くからの知己であり、こ

they have exerted on the conduct of life. Not only in the usages of polite society, but also in the arrangement of all our domestic details, do we feel the presence of the tea-masters. Many of our delicate dishes, as well as our way of serving food, are their inventions. They have taught us to dress only in garments of sober colours. They have instructed us in the proper spirit in which to approach flowers. They have given emphasis to our natural love of simplicity, and shown us the beauty of humility. In fact, through their teachings tea has entered the life of the people.

Those of us who know not the secret of properly regulating our own existence on this tumultuous sea of foolish troubles which we call life are constantly in a state of misery while vainly trying to appear happy and contented. We stagger in the attempt to keep our moral equilibrium, and see forerunners of the tempest in every cloud that floats on the horizon. Yet there is joy and beauty in the roll of the billows as they sweep outward toward eternity. Why not enter into their spirit, or, like Liehtse, ride upon the hurricane itself?

He only who has lived with the beautiful can die beautifully. The last moments of the great tea-masters were as full of exquisite refinement as had been their lives. Seeking always to be in harmony with the great rhythm of the universe, they were ever prepared to enter the unknown. The "**Last Tea of Rikiu**" will stand forth forever as the acme of tragic grandeur.

Long had been the friendship between Rikiu and

の偉大な武将はこの茶人に一目置いていた。だが暴君の友であることほど危険な名誉はない。当時は裏切りが頻繁にあったため、だれもが最も近いものさえ信じられなくなっていた。利休は単なるご機嫌取りの家来ではなく、意見が違えば気の短い主君と議論を戦わすことも珍しくなかった。ときには秀吉と利休の仲が冷え込むこともあり、敵対するものはその機に乗じて、利休が秀吉毒殺の陰謀に加担していると非難を浴びせた。誰かが秀吉の耳に、利休が死に到る量の毒を入れた茶を点てて太閤殿に供するつもりだと吹き込んだ。そんな疑いだけで秀吉には十分だった。秀吉は直ちに利休の処刑を命じた。怒れる支配者の意思に逆らう道はない。とがめられた者に残された唯一の特権は、自らの手で死ぬ栄誉だけだった。

　**自害**の当日、利休は主だった弟子を集めて最後の茶会を催した。指定された刻限に、悲嘆にくれる弟子たちは待合に顔をそろえた。庭へ通じる小道に目を向けると、樹木は悲しみに震え、木の葉の擦れ合う音には亡霊たちのささやきがまじっている。灰色の石灯籠は、黄泉の国ハデスの入り口に立つ恐ろしい番人のようだ。珍しい香の香りが茶室から漂ってくる。客人たちの入室を促す合図だ。彼らは一人ずつ入っていき、それぞれの席に着く。床の間の掛け軸は昔の僧侶の手になる立派な書で、この世のものすべての**儚さ**を説いていた。炉に乗せた茶釜が沸き立ち歌

▶**黄泉の国ハデス**
　黄泉とは死者が住むと信じられた国。ハデスは、ギリシア神話で冥界の王を指す。

the Taiko-Hideyoshi, and high the estimation in which the great warrior held the tea-master. But the friendship of a despot is ever a dangerous honour. It was an age rife with treachery, and men trusted not even their nearest kin. Rikiu was no servile courtier, and had often dared to differ in argument with his fierce patron. Taking advantage of the coldness which had for some time existed between the Taiko and Rikiu, the enemies of the latter accused him of being implicated in a conspiracy to poison the despot. It was whispered to Hideyoshi that the fatal potion was to be administered to him with a cup of the green beverage prepared by the tea-master. With Hideyoshi suspicion was sufficient ground for instant execution, and there was no appeal from the will of the angry ruler. One privilege alone was granted to the condemned—the honour of dying by his own hand.

On the day destined for his **self-immolation**, Rikiu invited his chief disciples to a last tea-ceremony. Mournfully at the appointed time the guests met at the portico. As they look into the garden path the trees seem to shudder, and in the rustling of their leaves are heard the whispers of homeless ghosts. Like solemn sentinels before the gates of Hades stand the grey stone lanterns. A wave of rare incense is wafted from the tearoom; it is the summons which bids the guests to enter. One by one they advance and take their places. In the tokonoma hangs a kakemono,—a wonderful writing by an ancient monk dealing with the **evanescence** of

い出す。まるで過ぎゆく夏を惜しむ蝉の声のようだ。やがて利休が入ってくる。一人ひとり、順番に茶が供され、一人ひとりが無言で飲みほしていく。最後は利休。伝統の作法に従い、客人の長が茶器の検分の許しを乞う。利休は皆の前にさまざまな道具を置く。掛け軸も置く。皆がその美しさを口々に讃え、利休は客の一人ひとりに１品ずつ形見分けする。利休の手元には茶碗だけが残った。


「不運な唇によって汚されたこの茶碗が、二度と使われぬように」利休はそう言って、その茶碗を粉々に打ち砕いた。

茶会は終わった。客人たちはあふれ出す涙をこらえ、最後の別れを告げて茶室を出ていく。一人だけ、最も近しい者だけが求められて残り、最後を見届けることになる。利休は茶会の衣装を脱ぎ、きちんとたたんで畳に置く。もはや身につけているのは純白の死に装束のみ。利休は刀の白刃を静かにみやり、辞世を詠む。


きたれ、
永遠（とわ）なる剣よ！
仏陀を貫き
達磨（だるま）をも貫き、
汝は汝の道を貫くがいい

all earthly things. The singing kettle, as it boils over the brazier, sounds like some cicada pouring forth his woes to departing summer. Soon the host enters the room. Each in turn is served with tea, and each in turn silently drains his cup, the host last of all. According to established etiquette, the chief guest now asks permission to examine the tea-equipage. Rikiu places the various articles before them with the kakemono. After all have expressed admiration of their beauty, Rikiu presents one of them to each of the assembled company as a souvenir. The bowl alone he keeps.

"Never again shall this cup, polluted by the lips of misfortune, be used by man." He speaks, and breaks the vessel into fragments.

The ceremony is over; the guests with difficulty restraining their tears, take their last farewell and leave the room. One only, the nearest and dearest, is requested to remain and witness the end. Rikiu then removes his tea-gown and carefully folds it upon the mat, thereby disclosing the immaculate white death robe which it had hitherto concealed. Tenderly he gazes on the shining blade of the fatal dagger, and in exquisite verse thus addresses it:

> *Welcome to thee,*
> *O sword of eternity!*
> *Through Buddha*
> *And through Dharuma alike*
> *Thou hast cleft thy way.*

こうして利休は、笑みを浮かべて彼岸へと旅立ったのだ。

第7章　茶　人